# JUSTICE CHURCH

# JUSTICE CHURCH

*The New Function of the Church
in North American Christianity*

*Frederick Herzog*

ORBIS BOOKS

Maryknoll, New York 10545

Second Printing, July 1981

The Catholic Foreign Mission Society of America (Maryknoll) recruits and trains people for overseas missionary service. Through Orbis Books Maryknoll aims to foster the international dialogue that is essential to mission. The books published, however, reflect the opinions of their authors and are not meant to represent the official position of the society.

Library of Congress Cataloging in Publication Data

Herzog, Frederick.
  Justice church.

  Includes bibliographical references.
  1. Theology—20th century. 2. Church. 3. Liberation theology. I. Title.
BT28.H43      261      80-15091
ISBN 0-88344-249-3 (pbk.)

FOR THE UNITED CHURCH OF CHRIST
and all other
North American denominations
struggling for the just church

*The Lord of hosts is exalted in justice.*
—Isaiah 5:16

*Seek first the kingdom of God and God's justice, and all other things shall be added unto you.*
—Matthew 6:33

*Perfect-paired as eagle's wings,*
*Justice is the rhyme of things.*
—Ralph Waldo Emerson

# Contents

# *Preface*

While these lines are being penned, guns are booming away in Nicaragua. My prayers these weeks have included Ernesto Cardenal on the side of the rebels. I also remembered Daniel Berrigan, who wrote to dissuade Cardenal from taking up arms. In these two names I have included all the people caught up in the struggle: No more Somozas, God, no more dictators.

During the writing of this book the realization was inevitable that there is a painful difference between the turmoil in Third World countries and our relatively tranquil ways in the First World. Does the difference mean that we do nothing at all in the liberation struggle? We cannot simply sit back and watch Third World people fighting the battle for us on our TV screens. The linkage between the United States and Nicaragua is only too obvious when we recall that the United States government provided for the Somoza regime from the very beginning. Our responsibility as a people is clear.

In August 1975 the "Theology in the Americas" Conference in Detroit brought us into closer contact with those leaders who bear much of the theological brunt of the Latin American liberation struggle. I will always remember the work of Father Sergio Torres in our midst. Our vision of what is happening in North America in the liberation struggle was greatly changed by his presence. Gustavo Gutiérrez, José Miranda, Leonardo Boff, José Míguez Bonino, and others appeared among us because of his efforts. We got to know them as persons.

Taking their presence seriously we realized that we had to continue to fashion our own tools in the struggle. We have been compelled to be as truthful about our own identity in the struggle as they are about theirs.

So I especially cannot forget Orbis Books which has made the printed page labor for the creative encounter between the northern and southern parts of the hemisphere—and not only of our hemisphere. Orbis Books has been able to call to wider public attention all the name Maryknoll has stood for already for scores of years. The ecumenical movement is being more advanced by its labors than by many an ecumenical conference.

What our sisters and brothers suffering under infinitely more difficult conditions feel about our effort matters greatly. But it matters even more that we are up-front with ourselves. We need to come clean with our own theological histories. Probably there will be some in this country (and elsewhere) who will miss inflammatory language in this book. Others will find it there. I cannot help it. What we badly need right now is cool reasoning about what our theological histories demand as the next realistic step in the North American liberation struggle.

The cover of the book reflects something of the spirit in which it was begun. When we started to meet in 1970 in the South on matters of liberation theology it was Merle Creech of Ocracoke, North Carolina, who provided the first sketches of the clenched fist "ending up" holding the Cross. Her work was continued by Kathy Snyder of Oklahoma City, who in 1971 offered her version of the design as it now appears on the cover. As we humans measure time, the red color has only of late turned into the color of secular revolution. It was first the color of God's revolution in Resurrection and Pentecost. This is what liberation theology in North America centrally struggles with: God's liberation focused in Cross and Resurrection.

In the Spirit of world-shaking Pentecost, the book is not tuned to "winning friends and influencing people." However, there is often more community in confrontation—including theological confrontation—than in shaking hands all around and singing "Heavenly Sunshine." In our divinity school and seminary culture we are living in a Fool's Paradise more often than in the real world. Harsh confrontation cannot hurt. It might wake us up.

The one thing I have tried to steer clear of is the hermeneutic of suspicion. In our money-mad competitive culture most of us are suspicious of each other anyway. What we need to struggle for is a clearer grasp of data on which to act. So instead of a hermeneutic of suspicion the book wants to foster a "hermeneutic of volition."

Whoever wills to do God's will, this person shall know whether this justice teaching is from God, or whether I speak on my own authority (cf. John 7:17). God's will is expressed in the poetry of the Gospel, opening up new dimensions for the imagination.

I see only too clearly the drawbacks of thinking about these things in an affluent society. But we have to take the risk. The alternative is walking corpses.

The principal thrust of the book is the attempt to develop a new theological method that can overcome the systems of a controlling reason still prevalent in the church. The process also involves rethinking our histories in the North American church. Above everything else we need to learn theological decontrol without giving up critical reason. That inevitably makes us labor over a new methodology.

As much as we may stretch our souls to be engaged in God-walk more so than God-talk, we still face the tragic paradox of human life. We fearsomely fall short of perfection. In all our efforts we cannot but fail, even in the best God-walk, if God's own liberation does not sustain us.

It is impossible to thank adequately all who over the years have helped to shape these pages. Some names will appear shortly on another page. Here I have to state that Paul Lehmann's influence has remained strong. I have had to launch out in directions he could often only frown at. But I know what it means to be indebted to a great teacher. The final shape of the book would not have been possible without the cooperation of Reuben Sheares and Ralph Quellhorst of the United Church of Christ Office for Church Life and Leadership and their permission to use the "Sound Teaching" document. Recently it has been translated into the German by Reinhard Groscurth and published in *Ökumenische Rundschau*, 28:3 (July 1979). Robert T. Osborn stood by faithfully in good and in bad days. Mary Chestnut patiently saw these pages through her typewriter, some more often than I care to admit. And my wife, Kristin, in her sterling ways made me weigh every word.

*F. H.*

# JUSTICE CHURCH

# Introduction

This work developed in an unexpected way. The harsh confrontations of the 1960s imposed on us a new datum of theology—one that triggered new queries. *Liberation Theology* (1972) was an attempt to address one of them. The book took its final shape in a small circle of struggling people in the South of the United States. Suddenly the horizon began to expand. Others throughout the country joined hands in the new effort.

Each chapter of this book reflects this expanding horizon. The first chapter took form in dialogue with fellow Christians in a Duke theology workshop, preparations for which began in 1974. The mere listing of names cannot adequately express my gratitude for the input of Thomas E. Ambrogi, Robert McAfee Brown, Lee Cormie, Paul Hammer, Edward M. Huenemann, Thomas A. Langford, M. Douglas Meeks, Lewis S. Mudge, Benjamin A. Reist, Theodore H. Runyon, George Telford, Robert W. Thornburg, and F. Thomas Trotter.

The last chapter grew in a different way. It is very much part of the same expanding horizon, though focused in large measure on the United Church of Christ (UCC). In 1976–77, the UCC Office for Church Life and Leadership convened a seminar to examine the present teaching mandate of the United Church of Christ. Again, I cannot pay adequate tribute to those whose contributions are reflected in this work. The vision of Walter Brueggemann, Paul Hammer, Ralph C. Quellhorst, Henry Rust, Reuben A. Sheares, James Smucker, Max L. Stackhouse, Clyde Steckel, and Peggy Way enlarged my own vision in writing this book. They offered the *telos*. I hope the report which appears in the Appendix will be used intensively in churches and theological seminaries.

Beginning in 1972 I have experienced a corporate accountability in the Christian community I had not known before. We feel responsible toward one another in tying theology to the life of the church in very concrete ways. The circle is still small, I know. But it cuts across the North American continent from East to West, and from North to South.

The chapters in this book exhibit the gradual growth in my understanding of the challenge of the church as Justice Church. The developing dialogue made me focus on the function of the church in the contemporary situation (Chapter One). That led to an examination of the function of the head of the church involving the beginnings of a new Christopraxis as ground of a new Christology (Chapter Two). Since the mainstream of North American modern theology seemed at odds with the new shape of things theological, I had to explain at least to myself why Friedrich Schleiermacher as "Father" of theological liberalism kept us from searching for the Justice Church (Chapter Three). Study in Schleiermacher's Berlin brought Karl Marx into close proximity to the beginnings of Protestant modernism. Marx turned out to be a painful antidote to liberal self-congratulation the modern churches of the West were only too eager to ignore (Chapter Four).

These factors have brought about a shift in the modernistic methodology of Protestantism. They impose on us a new hermeneutic of Christian origins (Chapter Five). In the course of my probings into these issues a new view of the function of the church gradually began to take shape (Chapter Six).

For a number of years it has been said that liberation theology has been the *bouleversement* of theological methodology. Now the results are in. The upshot of it all is a new view of the function of the church. It was in the taxing process of praxis, research, and dialogue that we finally got the point. The last "push" came at the 1977 American Academy of Religion meeting in San Francisco. Seven theologians had submitted a team paper on "Contextualization of Theology in the South."[1] Three blacks were involved, Thomas Hoyt, Jr., J. Deotis Roberts, Sr., and Henry J. Young. There were four whites, M. Douglas Meeks, Robert T. Osborn, Theodore Runyon, and myself. The discussion made it unmistakably visible that talking about liberation theology in general is self-defeating. The team paper was an exercise in "exorcism." The demons of false commitments and orientations were cast out. San Francisco 1977 hardened my resolve to face the relationship between theology and the church squarely.

## GOSPEL STORY AS PRAXIS TEXT OF THEOLOGY

It was the poor with the Bible in their hands who taught us liberation theology in the South. That is a simple fact. The first step was for us to discover that the Gospel pertains to the liberation of the poor as well as to the salvation of the soul. But that had to be thought through carefully, at least in regard to the Gospel story itself. *Liberation Theology* (1972) emerged from this process.

There has been much probing of "story" in theology in recent years. All this probing, however, can never evade the function of the Gospel story. All miracle stories and parables are seen to be within the framework of the Gospel story as a whole. It turns out that Christian theology has to be built around this framework if it wants to be Christian. The Gospel framework does not eliminate the theological significance of the New Testament epistolary literature or the Book of Revelation. It also does not do away with the relevance of the Old Testament. But Christian theology first of all has to make up its mind about the shape of Jesus' public ministry. That is predominantly witnessed to in the Gospel story.

Someone might object that there is in itself no more virtue in the shape of a life than in the weight of a thought. But the peculiar thing about Messiah Jesus is that for the church the new thought about God did not emerge via pure thought. In Messiah Jesus God acted out a way of being God unheard of before.

Obviously there was also thinking, hard thinking. But the hard thinking grew out of and was tied to a definite praxis. Jesus' praxis, we need to observe, gave rise to Christian thought. "Thinking on his feet," Jesus incarnated God. Thus praxis gives rise to thought.

What we need to understand is that unless we are intimately involved in the same matrix of human life in which Messiah Jesus incarnated God we cannot shape a Christian theology. The Gospel story is not primarily a talk-text, but a praxis-text. God-talk comes in God-walk. Involved in this ministry we begin to understand theology.

Dietrich Ritschl observes of stories in general: "Stories in their typical linguistic form of narration are not the expressive form but the raw material of theology."[2] In a broad sense, this is very much the case. The Gospel story, though, is the elementary expressive form as well as the elementary raw material of theology. It is in praxis that we find the expressive form of both Gospel and theology.

The Gospel story is the nucleus and basic framework of every Christian theology—on the level of praxis. It reflects Christopraxis.

## CHURCH AS PRAXIS CONTEXT OF THEOLOGY

This makes for the fundamental complication we are now struggling over at this juncture of theological research. Christian theology apparently cannot be done apart from the community of a particular praxis. It is not sufficient to say that Christian theology cannot be done apart from church. We need to discover together with the church that praxis which first of all shapes the church as church. The Gospel as framework of theology thrusts the theologian into the praxis of a peculiar type of community. It evokes the struggle for the new qualification of the church as Justice Church.

The praxis imperative dare not be understood in the abstract. Praxis is to be seen in terms of the shape of Jesus' public ministry. The significance of the figure of Jesus is not a sheer reduplication of the exodus, or anything else in the past. It is a new event with its own validity, not apart from Israel's history, but not simply repeating it either.

What is available to us of the originative event of Christianity is only the Gospel—language that actually does something with words. What this language does is quite unlike Schleiermacher's use of symbol. The Protestant modernistic view of Christianity made Messiah Jesus a cipher of a deeper or more comprehensive reality to which all of us have direct access. Neo-reformation theology, Barth foremost, tried to stop this transference of ultimate meaning courageously and with much vigor. But this attempt fell back upon Chalcedon's use of concept as the dominant form of Christian language.

What the Gospel as praxis text of theology brings out is the predominantly metaphorical character of Gospel language. It does not transfer meaning to a deeper or higher reality, nor does it primarily conceptualize reality. It creates new reality. In the light of the newly created reality, reality as a whole is questioned, acted upon, and interpreted in a new way.

Transformation of reality and interpretation of reality are not exclusive of each other. It is a question of priorities when it comes to the Gospel. It is often said that liberation theology demands the transformation rather than the interpretation of reality. The point is, however, that for the shape of Jesus' public ministry interpretation grows out of transformation.

The root-metaphors of the Gospel are Messiah Jesus and Jesus, Son of God. They are utterly transformative. What they effect will be more fully explicated throughout the book.

Christian theology turns out to be a constant dialogue with the momentum of the root-metaphors of the church in Christopraxis. Needless to say, anyone can pick up the Christian material and try to develop some theology for his or her personal satisfaction. But any such attempt is not specifically Christian theology. Responsible Christian theology is always an effort to give an account of the continuing activity of Messiah Jesus in his community. Just what that activity is can ultimately not be settled abstractly by theologians talking to each other, but only by Christians struggling together in the praxis of history.

It should be quite obvious that we are not advocating a withdrawal from society when we stress the church as praxis context of theology. We are zeroing in on the church immersed in the struggles of history. There is no point in developing a theology in general. The general public is not the addressee of a Christian theology. It does not need it. The Christian community needs it.

## PRAXIS TEXT ANALYSIS
## AND PRAXIS CONTEXT ANALYSIS

Charles R. Strain, in his article on "Ideology and Alienation: Theses on the Interpretation and Evaluation of Theologies of Liberation," suggests that "theologies of liberation are characterized by advocacy scholarship and passionate rhetoric in contrast to the philosophical rigor and conceptual precision typical of systematic reflection."[3] I do not think it makes sense to lump all liberation theologies together and to act as though they were a theological genre all by themselves. The whole idea of each liberation theology is to take seriously in a particular context analysis of the data for which Christian theology is responsible. That most liberation theologies turned to social analysis for help was because much previous theology had a blindspot when it came to the hermeneutical significance of the poor. Some dimensions of the praxis text had not been considered. One found in the text too much of what one had wanted to find. In that regard, each liberation theology initially took on a life of its own.

I believe it is fair to say that the first stage of liberation theology is behind us. Whoever does not now want to see the poor as part of the Gospel and consequently as a significant claim on us in hermeneutical decisions is probably willingly blinding herself or himself to them. Praxis text analysis is now followed by praxis context analysis. Both analyses are allied with "the philosophical rigor and conceptual precision typical of systematic reflection." Yet that alliance has to be brought out into the open more fully.

The six chapters of this book are an attempt at an analysis of the praxis context. Each chapter in itself presents a particular difficulty we have to contend with. The effort is not geared to answers. It is a second prolegomena volume of sorts. It wants to say that these are the tasks philosophical rigor and conceptual precision have to deal with in even more systematic reflection. The result is a new methodology for Protestant thought.

On one level, the first chapter confronts the false powerlessness of the church and the second chapter the reality of true powerlessness. The third chapter puzzles over the causes of the false powerlessness of liberal Protestantism, and the fourth chapter wonders about the supersession of a church failing to engage in the power struggle. Finally, the last two chapters highlight problems we face as we seek to work our way out of the dilemmas of modern Protestantism.

There are other levels in each of the individual chapters. But whatever the level, the book wants to say: these are a few of the major problems any future systematic theology has to tackle while in view of the poor Christ and the world's poor it develops a new methodology.

The challenge is to understand how in working on the new task we can become more just, that is, more human.

We cannot hope to achieve more than responsible theology.

## NOTES

1. Now published in *The Journal of Religious Thought*, 36:1 (Spring-Summer 1979), pp. 54–60.
2. Dietrich Ritschl and Hugh O. Jones, *"Story" als Rohmaterial der Theologie* (Munich, 1976), p. 41.
3. Charles R. Strain, "Ideology and Alienation: Theses on the Interpretation and Evaluation of Theologies of Liberation," *Journal of the American Academy of Religion*, 45:4 (December 1977), p. 476.

CHAPTER ONE

## Power Dilemmas in the Church

"The theology of our church stinks." This statement made recently by a layperson in Sunday School may seem unsavory. The honest truth for him was that we were doing a lot of good things in our church, but mostly for the wrong reasons. Our theology was no longer in touch with the real world.

For some time many of us have been telling ourselves: Our church is in trouble. But the reasons for the trouble have turned out to be different from what they had seemed.

Many of our churches still create an atmosphere of respectability. But they are living on borrowed capital, the memory of saintly souls, the spiritual aura still reflected in the religion sections of our newspapers, and the awe the label "Reverend" still exudes. So for awhile I concluded that what we are up against is a moral issue: respectability on Sunday, credibility gaps on Monday — in the real world.

At times we were able to close the credibility gap. But then there was also the role society assigned the church in the sociopolitical and socioeconomic power play. Society often expected the church to sanction its ways. This brought in a sociological dimension.

Neither the moral nor the sociological dimension, however, explains the dilemma fully. What is in bad shape is the basic doctrinal view of the church. While not unrelated to the moral and the sociological, the dilemma is concerned principally with how we see the church functioning in the global village. What we have thought of as church thus far is one thing. What it needs to be in the global village is quite another.

We are no longer living in the age of universal Christendom. The Constantinian era is over. The church is no longer the sacred

8

center of society. But what is it? The new function of the church is still developing.

## THE OLD CONCEPT OF THE CHURCH?

Of the acme of Christendom Juan Luis Segundo claims: "The Church was universal because all men belonged to her. The chief byproduct of this view was that missionary activity ceased to be the task of *each* and *every* Christian. The pagan was no longer someone you lived with or near; in a Christian world there were no pagans, just good or bad Christians. The pagan was someone living beyond the borders of the West, specifically in the Islamic world challenged by holy crusades."[1] That has changed radically. Pagans are again in our midst. But the change has not been fully grasped as yet. The churches are still widely regarded as integrative centers of holiness in terms of an American Christendom. The idea of a civil religion implies no less.

Countless laypersons as well as clergy are trying to break out of the old mold. Almost daily our newspapers carry items to that effect. In the case of foreign policy, for instance, the question has once again been raised, "What do we do in the face of increasing Soviet power?" Speaking from a Christian perspective Father Theodore M. Hesburgh, chairperson of the Overseas Development Council, observed that "the emphasis today tends to be distracted to political problems, like . . . how strongly we speak to the Russians." He believes we should rather be discussing "the place of America in a world in which we're surrounded by great concentrations of poverty and hopelessness."[2]

The abandonment of the old vision of the church has led to new conflicts in the churches. For years the developing polarity has been summed up in the formula: the church as challenger vs. the church as comforter.[3] Only gradually is it dawning on us that the struggle over the nature of the church is over the church immersed in history vs. the church separate from history.

Thus far in the debate we have usually talked about the conflict between a more liberal and a more conservative view of the church. The liberal view often still sees the church as an end in itself, conceptually at least, existing apart from the vicissitudes of history. The theology of Paul Tillich may still function as a test case in regard to liberal U.S. Protestant thought. Here for the last time a liberal theologian in this country has taken it upon himself to restate the western ontological tradition on a grand scale.

Tillich's doctrine of the church appears within the ontological framework. He speaks of the "ontological character of the Spiritual Community."[4] Since Tillich wants to stress the church as the bearer of the New Being, he first describes what *is*. The sacramental character of the church is implied and a dual dimensionality becomes operative, a visible reality dimension, on the one hand, and a depth dimension, on the other. The latter does not meet the eye and yet accounts for the real nature of the church.

So, for a good stretch of the way, the challenge becomes how to put two churches together, the existential church and the essential church. We are familiar with the basic argument: "The Spiritual Community does not exist as an entity beside the churches, but it is their Spiritual essence, effective in them through its power, its structure, and its fight against their ambiguities." What we are faced with as church is people trying to draw more and more spirituality into reality. But that is not an easy thing to do. And so Tillich ends up with paradox: "The churches are holy, but they are so in terms of an 'in spite of' or as a paradox." Therefore a big issue for Tillich is how the churches can prove their mettle in terms of expressing Being.

Tillich's doctrine of the church appeared at a time when Gibson Winter and Peter Berger, among others, were already developing sociological critiques of the American churches. Within this new context, Langdon Gilkey published the important study on *How the Church Can Minister to the World Without Losing Itself* (1964). Gilkey's concern was that the transcendent dimension, the Holy, was being lost in the shallow secularization process rampant in the American denominations. He was searching for a new language that could once more capture "the dimension of transcendence or of the holy in the church's life." In some sense that might have seemed like holding on to the ontology of the church the way Tillich had seen it. And yet, in principle, Gilkey's study was a first step in a new direction. What Gilkey really thought important was an analysis "of the actual social community we label church." The advance was related to his contention that theological language, whether denominational or ecumenical, "has seemed to refer to some other church than the actual one."[5] Gilkey was also very much aware of his limitations. He expressed the hope "that far better historical and theological analyses will replace this brief one."

Our analysis does not pretend to be better than Gilkey's. Rather it attempts simply to take into account a few developments since the time of Tillich's and Gilkey's contributions. Our effort will be based on a premise already important to Gilkey: *In our day we need to be keenly aware of the shift from theologizing about an ideal church to analyzing the actual church.*

## A NEW CONCEPT OF THE CHURCH?

It is beginning to dawn on us that the church exists not apart from history, but in the rough and tumble of history. The result is a turning away from apologetics, in other words, from the primary attempt to convince the elites of the logical consistency of Christianity. We are discovering in the world countless people who do not have the privilege of being part of the modern mind: the non-persons, that is, the marginals, the voiceless poor. It is not so much that *we* are discovering them, as that they are imposing themselves on us as persons no longer to be overlooked. The nature and mission of the church needs now to be formulated in regard to our inability thus far to make creative use of this new situation in which non-persons are making claims on us.

With full awareness of the problem Gilkey was trying to tackle, I tried almost a decade later to tie theology to the claims of the victims of society:

> The church is never an end in itself. . . . Its task is to witness to transcendence. . . . Insofar as it does point to transcendence, God's involvement in the wretched of the earth, it is the liberation church. . . . To admit that God struggles among the oppressed means to join the battle in opening up public space for freedom for those who have no access to it.

Opening up white churches for black members makes little difference for those who suffer. The real point is to open jobs and better housing. On a wider scale it is granting unionization rights to *Chicanos* and self-determination to Vietnamese."[6]

While the church here is understood no longer as a *community* alongside history, but as a people joining God in the liberation struggle in history, it is not at all clear in detail how a local church might go about embodying this new concept.

The organizational framework in which the churches exist cannot give credence to this new insight. We need a different organizational structure. This is not meant to be another move in "modern" culture-accommodation. It is rather an effort to grasp what the Christian movement is all about *on its own grounds.*

The theological point seems fairly clear. In Jesus of Nazareth something happened outside the temple. After death and resurrection the story is carried beyond the temple to the pagans. Worship of God as the Holy can no longer be confined to temples made with hands. God proved to be struggling with all humanity, especially those who had been excluded from being human. People in the Gentile world had been battling for solutions to their historical destiny. Greek mystery religions and Greco-Roman philosophers were no longer providing satisfactory answers. The enterprise of civilization was grinding to a halt. Especially the lower classes felt the purposelessness of life. They were the "expendables." But Jesus included them. The church also included them and thus thrust itself deep into history.

Since that time, much has changed. Other parts of this book will try to give a more detailed account of the dimensions of the changes. Here we need to point out that insight into *the dilemmas of power in the church* does not spring directly from the new concept of the church like Athena from the head of Zeus. For example, H. Richard Niebuhr, as early as 1929, offered a good historical explanation of the dilemmas when he observed: "The same causes which brought on political and economic conflict promoted religious controversy and schism. For the churches of America, no less than those of Europe, have often been more subject to the influence of provincial or class environment than to the persuasions of a common gospel."[7] A European, Friedrich Hufendick, in recent reflection on H. Richard Niebuhr describes the result of this environmental influence: "The churches of the bourgeoisie have separate organizations aiding them in avoiding economic conflict between the classes."[8] But why did H. Richard Niebuhr not make headway with his insights? Why did he end up with a middle-of-the-road Schleiermacherian liberalism almost looking the other way in social conflict?

Who has a satisfactory answer? It seems as long as churches and theologians do not engage in a praxis that cuts across denominational lines the church is bound to fail. Individual mergers between denominations are usually gargantuan agonies over wedding the class-interests of one class of Christian people thus far separate. One result is bigger corporations. In the process Protestant theology continues either to plug into a separate denominational setting or it diffuses its energies in trying to be relevant to the general cultural context.

The denomination is one of the basic hindrances to an embodiment of a new concept of the church. And yet it is precisely here that we have to start anew, principally in terms of analysis. The denomination, once upon a time fulfilling the role of cultural homebase for the immigrant, has become a closed society — a prehistorical monstrosity. We know only faintly what is going on in a denomination not our own. As a consequence, theology suffers immeasurably. For example, those of us who are not Presbyterians probably know more about Communist politics in Italy than about the United Presbyterian Church (UPCUSA).

John R. Fry recently published *The Trivialization of the United Presbyterian Church,* a study of the UPCUSA from the Confession of 1967 to the present. The struggle of our sister denomination this past decade did not remain entirely unknown to us on the outside. But how can we adequately judge the agony of this Presbyterian author? Fry is struck by the disproportion between the 1967 confession of reconciliation and the actual historical role of present church dilemmas. Our Presbyterian sisters and brothers went through a radical restructuring of the bureaucracy supposedly in keeping with the confession of reconciliation. Fry views the process as an exercise in futility: "The reorganizational effort grew a life of its own; once in place as an actual organization, it tried to function in independence of existing denominational dynamics although it insists all along that it is the very incarnation of the Presbyterian spirit."[9] Thus trivialization increased. The intended UPCUSA impact on the world decreased: "The UPCUSA *has* retreated; moreover, it *has* retreated from a once considerable and highly visible ministry to the nation into a ministry to itself."[10]

We have no way of adequately judging the truth of Fry's analysis from the outside. In "God's country" Christians are kept at a distance from each other. Most theology exists only in the awkward gaps between denominational pains and trials. When one member suffers, we do not suffer along by a long shot. Many Protestant Christians in the United States are increasingly retreating into a ministry to themselves. We are kept from battling in concert in the conflict of history by self-serving denominational machinery. This is perhaps the major reason why theology in the United States today is in such dire straits. Theology cannot flourish in closed societies. The common praxis from which alone liberation theology can grow has been hermetically sealed off by the churches themselves. But we cannot hope to develop a new praxis base alongside the churches. Uprooted from the church, theology always turns into something different from *Christian* theology. So, theologically speaking, we had better take our existence as separate denominations seriously.

The constant complaint that "it's off season" for the ecumenical movement can best be explained in this context.[11] For awhile the cerebral Faith and Order differences between the denominations seemed a good conversation piece. The trade flourished. Meanwhile, the differences have either been ironed out or gone up in smoke. At least they no longer grip the imagination. All the while the plight of the world's poor is growing and the plight of the churches as well.

This does not mean that all problems are confined to the area of Life and Work. There is a wholeness to the present church mandate that can best be grasped as *praxis seeking understanding*. Praxis gives rise to thought. So we cannot understand the ministry of the

church apart from the praxis interdependence of the denominations. Obviously one can try to go it alone. But that becomes more
and more absurd. Thus we arrive at a first principle in regard to a
liberation doctrine of the church: *From now on it will be absurd to try
to carry out the ministry of the church in abstraction from interdenominational praxis.*

## DIVIDE AND CONQUER?

While interdenominational praxis cooperation is occasionally
taking place in broad terms, we dare not forget that the U.S.
churches are also divided by race. After the emancipation of the
slave, dealing with the race problem in terms of denominational
pluralism was the safest way to keep the U.S. socioeconomic and
sociopolitcal system intact. The situation today remains very
much the same. The debate about black theology that raised so
many eyebrows obviously was an event triggered by the racial
apartheid involved in denominational pluralism.

One of the first attempts to overcome apartheid in the South
centered on the notion of "becoming black." The emphasis was
not placed for shock value.[12] There was a shock effect, it cannot
be denied, but this was an unexpected by-product. Originally it
meant (in Christian humor) white Christians discovering the in-
clusive structure of human selfhood in Jesus of Nazareth. As the
debate developed, we learned that in the church pluralism functions as camouflage for racism. The other side of the coin is that
pluralism in the church often also provides the occasion for ethnic
nationalism, which, in the end, is part of the power dilemma.

The issue has not as yet fully crossed the threshold of theological consciousness in Protestantism. Since I have become part of
the debate, I would like to refer to a few comments of Donald G.
Shockley which reflect the popular response to the issue. In a
review of Benjamin A. Reist's *Theology in Red, White, and Black*,
Schockley wrote:

> Reist begins to make the tired word "liberation" meaningful
> for all of us. Until now liberation has implied for whites
> some kind of escape from their whiteness, e.g., Frederick

Herzog's *Liberation Theology*. For Reist liberation means that whites at last come to terms with *their* particularity, i.e., become white for the first time. The conversation around the theological triangle requires the presence of white theologians who are willing to sit on *their* side of the triangle and participate as equals, no more nor less.[13]

There is a misunderstanding involved. We cannot escape from whiteness ever. We never intended an escape. The point was to become aware of our separate identities in the corporate selfhood of Christ.

The real intention was stressed by AME Bishop Philip R. Cousin: "As we see it, exactly in 'becoming black' (identifying with the black in our common history) whites can wish only one thing, namely to be white, that is, to be what they are. This new experience has the strange effect of making whites more conscious of themselves as whites. In the same vein, it should be noted that Herzog also spoke of becoming red, identifying with the Indian. The issue of our common history in North Carolina has at least this 'triadic' dimension."[14] In the South we learned years ago that only because of the confrontation with the black *and the red* could the issue of "becoming white for the first time" be raised. Solutions, however, are not easy to come by. It is a sad commentary on our complacency when we assume we can already sit around tables as equals with blacks and reds. Equals we will not be for a long time. Racism runs too deep. And we whites know it: we have the power.

Has anything been gained by this discussion? In the black/white/red confrontation we have become aware of the subtle "victory" of the social system over the church. We now see the great distance between us, basically a societal one. At times the evil distance due to racism is turned into the virtue of ethnic pluralism. On this level, though, we discover ourselves even more radically out of each other's reach. Pluralism due to racism is totally negative. Pluralism legitimating ethnic nationalism is often viewed as positive. But what does it do to Christianity? Even the seemingly good dimension of ethnic nationalism pits us against each other — just what the social system wants, to keep us in rivalry with one another.

Ethnic nationalism proves a positive good only when measured by the pluralistic ideology of our society. Ethnic pluralism as much as denominationalism is a codeword for rugged individualism or even social Darwinism. Illusions are no longer possible in the church on this point. Because of the racial confrontation in the theology of the late sixties and early seventies our eyes have been opened to the great distance still existing between the various nationalisms of the churches. The sociocultural system ultimately determines who we are as human beings, not the church. This is the way sociocultural power functions in the United States.[15] We can be churches in terms of our various nationalisms, but we cannot be the *United* Church of Christ. Obviously several denominations have "alien" ethnic groups within their folds. But that is no solution to the dilemma. The ethnic group in a denomination usually still functions as an ethnic nationalism inside a denomination and intentionally so. Those who have the power can thus more easily rule — as they divide us against each other.

Harold Cruse makes the significant point that America is a group society. So we need to think of this nation primarily in groups. While the overall economic principle remains the same, it uses ethnic groups to inject itself ever deeper into the body politic: "Negro workers, just like white workers, adopt the individualistic ideas of free enterprise and accept its values."[16] In order to understand our peculiar difficulties we have to view society "more cogently in terms of groups than in what the Marxist called class alignments."[17] Thus Cruse concludes: "The Negro question, contrary to Marxist dogma, is more a group problem than a class one, simply because Negro businessmen must depend on the Negro group for their support, regardless of class differentiation."[18]

Cruse offers his comment on the basis of research into "five decades of Marxism"[19] in the black community. One of the reasons why socialism is unable to make much of a dent among blacks in the United States is that the oppressed are boxed into ethnic groups and would be sold down the river if they would follow Marxist advice and integrate into a national multicolored class. The U.S. Marxist "class" would consist of ethnic groups continuing to seek domination within the overall competitive framework of our society. Says Cruse: "It has come to this! At its roots the American nationality problem is a group power problem, an interethnic group power play; only when the American Negro creates an ethnic group social and cultural philosophy will he be able to deal effectively with this dilemma in real terms."[20] The reasoning is not beside the point. The ethnic nationalisms are a parallel to the nationalisms of the international labor movement prior to World War I. The creed of international solidarity in the laboring class broke down as soon as national allegiance became the decisive factor at the outbreak of the war. The labor movement as an international movement has not recovered since. The dynamics operative there is also at work among us.

The poor or oppressed in our society are prevented from becoming an effective class by ethnic nationalism. The same is true of the poor and oppressed in the churches. That's how our system works. It has perfected the "divide and conquer" rule by which the high and the mighty have always controlled dissent.[21] In our context ministry here is up against its greatest limitation. Interethnic praxis is next to impossible in the churches.

Thus we arrive at the second principle of a liberation doctrine of the church: *Since interethnic praxis is next to impossible at this time, and yet ministry is unifying activity among humankind, ministry turns into subversive activity in the United States today.*

## WHAT DARE THE CHURCH THINK AGAIN?

Ministry becomes subversive where it opposes the church as a mirror of the present state of American culture, especially the various pluralisms that sustain the division of the churches. There is no reason to think of a subversive ministry as a sign of megalomania. Methodism, for example, has a good record of subversive ministry. Wrote Bishop Asbury in his *Journal* for December 26, 1806: "The work of God is wonderful in Delaware. But what a *rumpus* is raised. We are subverters of government — disturbers of society — movers of insurrections. Grand juries in Delaware and Virginia have presented the noisy preachers —

lawyers and doctors are in arms — the lives, blood, and livers of the poor Methodists are threatened: poor, crazy sinners! see ye not that the Lord is with us."[22] With this kind of tradition, should Methodism be surprised if the same thing happens in its ranks today? The church always seems to get caught in the fangs of culture. Let us take Methodism as an example of what is happening in a U.S. denomination. A good focus is a paper authored by John B. Cobb and published by the United Methodist Board of Higher Education and Ministry.

John B. Cobb, while realizing that the "concrete life of the church largely reflects the society and culture of which it is a part," wonders whether or not the church can "enter into and advance the frontiers of Western thinking."[23] His considerations take place under the aegis of "Can the Church Think Again?" Cobb uses liberation theology as one of the foils of his argument:

> There are others who see little importance in the internal life of the church. They are concerned that the church's energies be mobilized for social reform or the liberation of the oppressed. Among the liberation theologians, some *are* sharing in the cutting edge of thought insofar as that thought is the ideology of repressed groups seeking freedom. If the basic condition of the church were healthier, their leadership might become significant. But we can hardly expect to mobilize for sacrificial action in the world a community which does not experience its inherited faith as relevant to its own internal activities. And we can hardly expect persons outside the church to be moved by a prophetic word which cannot be heard within it."[24]

There is a shifting of focus going on here. Liberation theology, as I understand it, has indeed directed itself to "the internal life of the church." Perhaps during the past decade when, according to Cobb, the church got accustomed to getting along without thinking, some of us thought along lines *not approved as thinking* by some academic theologians. The impression is given by Cobb that all along we have known the theological subject. What we have failed to do is to tie it "into the current state of cultural and intellectual

life of the West." But what about theological amnesia among the
theologians as to their real subject matter? Might there not be a
great difference between Cobb's apologetic interest, "sharing in
the cutting edge of thought"[25] today, and the specific theological
task? Could it not be really unthinking for theology right now not
to do specifically *theo*logical thinking? What about the claims *God*
makes on us through the poor as we are caught in our denominational power dilemmas?

Besides the struggle between the "truth" of the church and the
untruths and truths of the western world, there is also the
theological struggle over truth and untruth in the church itself,
the issue of apostasy and heresy. The way I read Cobb, he implies
that sharing in the ideology of nonchurch groups is what needs to
be done. In liberation theology a few of us do not in the least
intend to share in the *ideology* of repressed groups as the foundation of theology. It is rather a question of discovering the reality of
God in Messiah Jesus. Here *God's* praxis happens to include
oppressed groups: "Blessed are you poor" (Luke 6:20).

The crucial task for theology is to make clear why God's praxis
is not as yet becoming relevant to the "internal activities" of the
church. In a church that mirrors the pluralism of culture God's
praxis in Messiah Jesus is effectively locked out. People in the
churches become agents of the countervailing power pluralism of
society. The impossibility of interethnic praxis in the churches is
partly due to the fact that society keeps Christians apart in
hermetically sealed denominations. The church has no power
left to determine its own internal activities. It no longer controls
its own life. The task of thinking in theology today is to clarify why
a prophetic word cannot be obeyed in the church.

What happens to power in a praxis that shares in God's praxis?
A theology that takes into account only the educated, the cultured, or the elites as its hermeneutical starting point has a hard
time serving him who "has nowhere to lay his head" (Matt. 8:20).
The New Testament tried to think through the power dilemmas
of the poor as well as the worries of the rich. While not excluding
the rich from God's concern, the New Testament church was
struggling hard to keep witnessing to God's identification with the
poor and the lost. I am not assuming that we already know what

all this entails for being a Christian today. But it appears that we first of all have to think through what exercise of power God's praxis in Christ demands before we can hope to tie effectively into any cultural trend of the West today.

Can the church think again? Is not the more adequate question — in the light of God's praxis — *what dare* the church think again? We are constantly misled by the false assumption that we already know what to think. If we think through God's praxis in our church context we learn that sharing in the internal activities of the church means focusing theology on the internal power vacuum in the church. Thus we arrive at a third principle of the liberation doctrine of the church: *Cultural pluralism imported into theology is the Trojan horse that destroys the internal life of the church, keeping us at war with each other in the church, and at a safe distance from real history.* It does not let us see history as the place where God struggles for justice.

## THEOLOGICAL EDUCATION AS CRUCIBLE?

Unless theological education as a whole can be reoriented, theological interest-group pluralism, reflecting society's countervailing powerplay, will continue to undermine theology from within. Obviously in trying to rectify a power dilemma of this magnitude we cannot do all things at once. The tendency to think of "two churches," referred to in the beginning of the chapter, still shows in even very progressive approaches to the doctrine of the church today. We need to see how the church cannot be the church in history as long as the power dilemma is disregarded, that is, as long as the internal activities of the denomination are not examined from the viewpoint of God's involvement in history. As long as the church is so structured that it cannot be involved the way God is involved in history there is no point in entering into or advancing the frontiers of western thinking.

Much theological education is still under the influence of the Niebuhr study of the fifties. Niebuhr speaks of the ministry twenty years ago as the "perplexed profession." Almost immediately he can tie this to the confusion of the church itself: "The contemporary church is confused about the nature of the ministry. Neither ministers nor the schools that nurture them are guided by a clear-cut, generally accepted conception of the office of the ministry, though such an idea may be emerging."[26] A clear-cut, generally acknowledged conception of ministry has in fact not emerged since. From observation of U.S. seminaries and churches Niebuhr called for what he thought was the newly emerging ministry-image, the "pastoral director." He was intrigued by the office from which the minister was directing the activities of the church. Niebuhr makes much of the place that determines how the minister functions: "The place in which the minister functions always signalizes the Church's idea of his task."[27] He was very sensitive to the dual history orientation accompanying the notion of the pastoral director:

> Today there is uncertainty about the ministry in Church and world partly because it is not clear whether the Church is fundamentally inclusive or exclusive, whether therefore the minister's concern is to extend to all in his reach or only to the faithful elite. Is the rural, the suburban, the inner-city, the college minister a parish person or a builder of a separated community? Is the theological teacher a minister of a separate ecclesiastical science or of a university subject?[28]

The internal activities of the church are not looked at in a level-headed fashion. It is not seen that there is no place for a separate community. The tasks of the church are the tasks of history — because of God's involvement. The task of the theological teacher is neither a separate ecclesiastical science nor a university subject.

Theological education in the eighties has to cope with several contradictions. Foremost is the contradiction between the actual accommodation of the Christian faith to culture, which makes it impossible for the church to function as a community with an identity of its own, and the taxing demand for the Christian community to join God's own involvement in history. Christians are involved in history, but never notice it. We are so much involved in it that what shapes us is what culture and society are doing with history. Yet we ask little what God's involvement in history does to shape us.

The contradiction between our culture-accommodation as church and God's involvement in history is partly grounded in the contradiction between a historicist relationship to Jesus and a living relationship to God's work in Christ in present history. In his analysis of theological education, H. Richard Niebuhr regards Jesus of Nazareth mostly as a historical figure to which we have a historical relationship. That reflects an overall attitude of much biblical scholarship. Practically this means that Jesus of Nazareth is safely removed from the present scene of history. Somewhat in the vein of H. Richard Niebuhr and taking the premises of the first fifty years of theology in the twentieth century into account, Van Harvey has developed a position that moves back and forth between (*a*) the historical Jesus and (*b*) the memory-image of Jesus. While acknowledging the historian's inability to outline a life of Jesus in detail, he lets the basic shape of Jesus' ministry come through as an orientation point for theological work. The basic yield of his reflection is the notion of Jesus as paradigm of awakening faith. Jesus' role was that "of having raised and answered the basic human question of faith. It was this role which made him the paradigm of God's action, for he had taught them to think of God as the one whose distinctive action is to awaken faith."[29] The whole paradigm function seems exhausted in God's call to *faith*.

It is not unimportant that Harvey sees Jesus as paradigm of *God*, not just of human existence. But he never draws out the positive strength of this emphasis. There is a specific warrant that accounts for Jesus as paradigm. Before Harvey outlines God's awakening of faith in Jesus he speaks of the distinctive characteristics of religious paradigms. Thus Jesus is part of Christianity as a *religion*, which functions as a common denominator of many expressions of faith, non-Christian as well as Christian. Once the common denominator has been announced, religion provides the basic matrix of understanding the memory-image of Jesus.

Harvey does not slight the *historical* character of the paradigmatic Christian events. They "do not direct the community away from history but have as their focus the life of responsibility in history."[30] Our peculiar responsibility in history, however, remains largely concealed. Harvey's religious catchall confuses things: "The basic concern was a religious one. Whether we may presuppose that the disciples came to this event with a religious question or whether the event itself raised the question for them we need not decide."[31] In Harvey everything is determined by the religious warrant. For religion it seems not very important to ask whether or not the event itself raised the question for the disciples. But this is the most crucial question: What does the event itself do to us? Does it raise a question different from the religious question?

Harvey is too careful a historian that he would not at least see other dimensions. But with the common denominator of religion they cannot become paradigmatic. He notices that Jesus "represents a radical reinterpretation of the concept of righteousness and of the ideas of God's power held by those who hoped to be justified by the law. Jesus consorts with the outcasts and the sick and the weak, those the 'righteous' call unrighteous."[32] What Harvey does not consider is whether Jesus' consorting with the outcasts is raising a paradigmatic question for us that cannot be subsumed under the general category of religion. The question of religion does not worry about a living relationship to God's work in Messiah Jesus in present history. Religion can leave Messiah Jesus in the past and do its own thing with God in the present. Here the contradictions in the contemporary church lie open before our eyes.

Theological education as crucible? A crucible is something "that tests as if by fire." What is being tested is our endurance in facing the contradictions. The internal activities of the church are being tested by God in Messiah Jesus in regard to a *radical reinterpretation* of righteousness. Since Jesus rose not just into the life of the church, and certainly not just into the kerygma, but into history, the challenge is to discover in what sense theology today can relate to the history into which Jesus rose as Lord.

God is still active in history in terms of Jesus' life. Practically this means that theological education will begin with the premise of praxis, not just with theory, doctrine, tradition, and ideas alone. What has been at stake all along this past decade has been hard thinking, thinking through in what sense each theological doctrine relates to the involvement of the Risen One in history. It does not mean in any sense an immediate call to action. The sociopolitical and socioeconomic problems we are facing are so vast we cannot hope to solve them by just wading into them. As we begin to act in terms of relating to history's sociopolitical and socioeconomic struggles *in which the church itself is caught,* we might be able, however, to become utterly aware of the present powerlessness of the churches and to begin to fight it with all our might.

Our present experience as Christians is dominated by the captivity of the churches in culture-accommodation. There are many Christians who by now grasp the contradiction between the captivity and God's involvement in history. Theological education often stays at a distance from the living God in history by concentrating on the historicist Jesus. That is, it stays in a safe realm of ideas. As soon as one turns from labeling Christianity a religion to a radical interpretation of God's righteousness, the praxis mandate cannot be avoided. We begin to understand God's righteousness as the *justice* that praxis seeking understanding is struggling for. What happens if one begins, not by modeling Christianity merely on a distant faith paradigm of the historical Jesus, but by relating it to historical reality today? We discover the poor. What we are being told by the poor in view of the Gospel is that theology grows out of praxis. Praxis gives rise to thought. And the first thought we think here is the powerlessness of the churches. The increasing pressures put on us by vast global structures, politically, economically, and technologically, are not effectively dealt with by the churches. The divided denominations are part of the problem. This is the most concrete form of the contradiction in which Christians live.

The old principle of theological education can only make Christians more religious. It practically means keeping the church apart from history. From now on theological education has to risk examining each doctrine or teaching in regard to the mandate of justice.

## PRAXIS SEEKING JUSTICE?

Theological education will grow responsible in new ways if it sees itself interlocked with the praxis tasks of the local church, especially in regard to liberty and justice for all. The contradictions in which theological education finds itself today are basically the same contradictions experienced in the local church. What the local church does not fully understand as yet is how it is tied into the power struggles of the global village. In many instances the local church does not even have an inkling of being accountable to the power play. Predominantly white mainline churches first need to discard the smokescreen of civil religion that still conceals the radical demands of justice.

Such a turning will be possible if theological education and Christian education can mutually inform each other in terms of forming the local church as an action/reflection group where the principles of our sudden awakening in the global village are thought through. This does not relegate worship or prayer to a secondary place. But the acts of service to God have to be seen much less exclusively as meditation or contemplation. There is not enough corporate social analysis informed by biblical analysis, not enough contemplation and celebration growing out of thoughtful involvement in concrete issues. The primary principle in every American is individual striving: "They would just make that little trip across the ocean! America — that's the country where a poor devil can get ahead."[33] But now there is a new principle: There is a global village where *all* poor devils need to get ahead. This fundamental shift in principle is not grasped as yet. We continue to disregard the exercise of power. We still act as though we were not limited by the global village.

There is nothing extremely difficult about the basic point. Theology and the church are met by the claims of the poor all over the world. The Gospel cannot be understood from the top down, only from the bottom up. Yet millions and millions of Christians are not close to the poor and do not want to get close. Someone might object that we cannot think of the poor all the time. But limits are inevitably imposed on us. We might as well face what is limiting us in the human family: not all people are in a physical condition to grasp the Gospel. They are too poor.

Our vision in the churches is not yet focused on our global village existence. The Gospel is still interpreted in terms of the *splendid isolation* of that "tiny island of Christianity" called the

United States. But can the Gospel still be understood at all in terms of such splendid isolation?

This book, then, is in large part an exercise in *new seeing*. It is a question of what we had better see in order to be responsible human beings. Since this is an attempt at seeing in the church, we are fundamentally asking what kind of church helps us in that seeing. No great vision of the future is offered. A few words of Peter L. Berger come to mind: "Our time is full of visions of the future, loudly and arrogantly proclaimed. Moral self-righteousness is evenly distributed throughout the political spectrum. . . . Yet they know so very little, all these self-confident prophets of doom and salvation. It is necessary to cultivate the quiet art of disbelief. It is necessary to act quietly and disbelievingly, out of compassion which is the only credible motive for any actions to change the world."[34] To this my response is: It is necessary to cultivate the quiet art of seeing. Without seeing the powerlessness and understanding the reasons for it, there can be no change in the church.

The task is a complex one. Pointing the finger does not aid insight. We will try to follow through the issue of power from Christian origins to the present in terms of several turns in outlook and attitude. Basically today in the United States we are up against a Leviathan of organization constantly interfering with clear thinking about what the church is called upon to do in regard to power. Arnold M. Rose has put the matter succinctly in claiming "not simply that power is pluralistic in American society, but that the society itself is pluralistic. The different spheres of life do not interpenetrate each other in the way in India, for example, religious values and institutions permeate the average man's political, economic, family, artistic, educational, and other spheres of life. . . . In the United States . . . practically every person has differentiated roles and values for the various spheres of life, and so power too usually does not significantly cross the boundaries of each sphere in which it is created."[35] The examination of power and powerlessness in the church involves a long thought-process. It makes us turn first of all to the head of the church and to analyze Christology in the face of power and powerlessness.

## NOTES

1. The difference in historical situations is very much the framework of Juan Luis Segundo, *Our Idea of God* (Maryknoll, 1974). See especially pp. 74–79.

2. Peter L. Berger, *Pyramids of Sacrifice* (Garden City, N.Y., 1976), is one of the best examples of what is happening in reorientation in the U.S. in this regard.

3. Jeffrey K. Hadden, *The Gathering Storm in the Churches* (Garden City, N.Y., 1969), p. 6.

4. Paul Tillich, *Systematic Theology*, III (Chicago, 1963). The quotes are taken from pp. 162ff.

5. Langdon Gilkey, *How the Church Can Minister to the World Without Losing Itself* (New York, 1964), p. 140.

6. Frederick Herzog, *Liberation Theology* (New York, 1972), pp. 22f.

7. H. Richard Niebuhr, *The Social Sources of Denominationalism* (New York, 1957), p. 140.

8. Friedrich Hufendick, "Von der Individualethik zur Gesell-schaftsethik," *Junge Kirche*, 6:1976, Beiheft, p. 6.

9. John R. Fry, *The Trivialization of the United Presbyterian Church* (New York, 1975), pp. 55f.

10. Ibid., p. 67.

11. Charles E. Brewster, "Off-Season for Ecumenism?" *New World Outlook*, 36:9 (May 1976), pp. 34–36.

12. Frederick Herzog, *Liberation Theology*, pp. 61ff.

13. Donald G. Shockley, review of Benjamin A. Reist, *Theology in Red, White and Black*, in *Religion In Life*, 44:4 (Winter 1975), p. 510.

14. Philip R. Cousin, "Black Identity and White Identity," in *Dialog*, 15:2 (Spring 1976), p. 148.

15. Cf. Arnold M. Rose, *The Power Structure: Political Process in American Society* (London, 1967), pp. 33ff.

16. Harold Cruse, *The Crisis of the Negro Intellectual* (New York, 1967), p. 157.

17. Ibid., p. 161.

18. Ibid., p. 174.

19. Ibid., p. 257.

20. Ibid., p. 260.

21. In understanding the dynamics of power in our society I have been much helped by Theodore J. Lowi, *The End of Liberalism: Ideology, Policy, and the Crisis of Public Authority* (New York, 1969).

22. Emory Stevens Bucke (ed.), *The History of American Methodism,* I (New York, 1964), p. 324.

23. John B. Cobb, "Can the Church Think Again?" *Occasional Papers: Issued by the United Methodist Board of Higher Education and Ministry,* 1:12 (August 9, 1976).

24. Ibid., p. 6.

25. Ibid.

26. H. Richard Niebuhr, *The Purpose of the Church and Its Ministry* (New York, 1956), p. 50. To bring change in this regard has been the intention of "Theological Education and Liberation Theology: An Invitation to Respond," *Theological Education,* 16:1 (Autumn 1979), pp. 7-11.

27. Niebuhr, *The Purpose of the Church,* p. 80.

28. Ibid., p. 75.

29. Van A. Harvey, *The Historian and the Believer* (New York, 1966), p. 270.

30. Ibid., p. 265.

31. Ibid., p. 270.

32. Ibid., p. 272.

33. O. E. Rölvaag, *Giants in the Earth* (New York, 1965), p. 218.

34. Peter L. Berger, *Pyramids of Sacrifice,* pp. 255f.

35. Arnold M. Rose, *The Power Structure: Political Process in American Society,* p. 33.

# CHAPTER TWO

## *Jesus and Power*

To address Christology today is something of a venture. We know most of the historical conditions that produced the creeds of the church. We are also aware of numerous historical circumstances that account for the shaping of the New Testament literature. It is obvious that there was a long and complex development from Peter's confession of Jesus' Messiahship (Matt. 16:16) to Chalcedon's formulas of the God-man.

For many Christians it is impossible today to repeat the creeds of the church without inquiring about the base in Christian origins that these creeds rely on. There is of course the pathetic move of playing off the simple Gospel against the Hellenistic creeds when there is nothing simple about the Gospel. We shall not fall into that trap. The real question is: What actually happened in Judaism to trigger a new faith movement called Christianity? The question has been asked many times before. But it has not as yet been pondered enough under the shadow of the decline of western theology.

"Whatever Happened to Theology?" was the question put by *Christianity and Crisis* to a number of theologians a few years ago.[1] The answers varied widely. But the question could not have been raised had there not been a feeling of a decisive change in western theology. That we all experience a "seismic shift" in theological orientation cannot be denied. Business as usual is passé. Western Christianity may have spent itself. It would be surprising if the decline of the West did not involve a decline of western Christianity and its theology.

For centuries Christianity in the West has been asking mainly two questions: (1) In what sense is Jesus the Christ? (2) In what sense is Jesus also God's Son? Perhaps, in the end, these are questions theology in the West will still be asking for centuries to come. But in this moment of change a long-neglected question also challenges us with irresistible force: What does it mean that Jesus was a Jew?

Obviously Jesus was not a Christian. But this factor is seldom given much attention. What happened in Judaism is, however, of great consequence, for it provided the basis for Hellenistic and Roman Christianity and later for western Christianity as a whole.

We also need to know the immediate pre-history of church history. What kind of sociocultural milieu did Jesus function in? What mainsprings of action were provided him by his society?

These questions, of course, have been asked in biblical studies all along. But it is surprising how little they are raised in systematic theology in regard to their doctrinal implications.

## GRAFTED INTO ISRAEL

Systematic theology quickly passes over the biblical context where the foregoing questions manifest their doctrinal import. Concerning the relationship of Gentiles to Jews, St. Paul, for example, tells the Romans: "But if some of the branches were broken off, and you, a wild olive shoot, were grafted in their place to share the richness of the tree, do not boast over the branches" (Rom. 11:17). The point is that the Gentile becomes part of Israel. Through faith in Jesus the Gentile becomes a Jew. I should not overstate the point. But according to the usual way of formulating the issue the Gentile needs to become a *Christian*. One consequence thereof is the frequent expectation that the Jew also must become a Christian.

The expectation that the Jew has to become a Christian is tied to Christianity as a cult religion where Jesus as the Christ has largely turned into a cult figure. Here Christian cult language explains itself through Christian cult language ad infinitum. That is what Christian theology tends to be all about in many quarters. But the systematic theologian needs first of all to understand the immediate pre-history of the Christian movement. The Old Testament is studied carefully by Christian scholars. What we need to consider in systematic theology is the significance of the fact that Jesus remained a Jew. We tend to overlook some things in the public ministry of Jesus. The strangest blindspot in systematic theology is the reason for his end on the cross. Much historical material needs to be sifted before one grasps the reasons for the trial resulting in a death sentence. Scholars are not in agreement as to what really happened. One thing we can all be certain of is that there was a power conflict between Jesus of Nazareth and those in authority. We often tend to overlook this because the cross has been integrated into Christianity as a cult religion. One focuses on its religious significance rather than on its historical causes.

Religion is a many-splendored tricky thing. One of its tricky aspects is mystification. It often is in the hands of wily professionals who exact tribute from a credulous following. In Jesus' day there were those in the lower class who were countering the professionals with their official myth and taking things into their own hands. The general mood is reflected in objections to the scribes and the Pharisees: "Woe to you, scribes and Pharisees, hypocrites! Because you shut the kingdom of heaven against men; for you neither enter yourselves, nor allow those who would enter to go in. . . . Woe to you, scribes and Pharisees, hypocrites! For you tithe mint and dill and cummin, and have neglected the weightier matters of the law, justice and mercy and faith" (Matt. 23:13, 23).

One cannot understand the pre-history of Christianity except as an internal struggle in Israel between those who had been disadvantaged by the religious professionals and the professionals themselves. This says nothing against Judaism as a whole. It means simply that in Judaism there were those with power and those who were powerless.

The struggle with the official myth of Israel created all kinds of intellectual and psychological tensions difficult to disentangle today. But it is altogether clear that the basic struggle was a power conflict over the *visio dei* and the *regnum dei*. It was a question of what all this history of Israel was finally coming to as regards the character of God and human selfhood.

In general terms, the New Testament vision of God as the

waiting God[2] or as costly love[3] will be readily acknowledged. But it is much less understood that the new view of God was interdependent with a new view of human selfhood. The full implications of both new dimensions were not immediately clear. It took nearly two thousand years of Christian history and countless experiments in interpretation to come to a small measure of understanding of only one of the dimensions. Especially unclear remained the human selfhood aspect. One has only to take a careful look at the creeds to see the point. Chalcedon, for example, worries about the *God*-man relationship and has little to say about who this man is who joins divinity and humanity in perfect union.

The blindspot pertains to the crucial factor in the power conflict in Jesus' public ministry. What upset the authorities was that unschooled persons took it upon themselves to work out the meaning of the official myth: " 'How is it,' they said, 'that this untrained man has such learning?' " (John 7:15). A little later we read: "The Pharisees retorted, 'Have you too been misled? Is there a single one of our rulers who has believed in him, or of the Pharisees? As for this rabble, which cares nothing for the Law, a curse is on them" (John 7:47–49).[4] The blindspot theme is here clearly articulated: the powerful and the rabble. For the Pharisees, according to this report, there were persons and nonpersons. Some belonged to a worthy ingroup, others were sheer rabble—white trash.

The challenge is to get deep into Judaism in this regard — and not just into "Christian Christology." The God encounter is here first of all tied to a particular Covenant context. Within this context something happened among non-persons that might be as paradigmatic for human history in the West as Chalcedon.

## A WESTERN PARADIGM

Among the many interpretations of Jesus of Nazareth in the West, much of the major concern has centered in cross and resurrection. This is especially true of the Protestant tradition, particularly the more recent giants of Protestant theology of whom Bultmann and Barth are perhaps the most representative.

In Bultmann's famous demythologizing essay it soon becomes

clear that the Jesus he is focusing on is the crucified Jesus who "bears vicariously the sin of the world, and by enduring the punishment for sin on our behalf . . . delivers us from death."[5] This mythological view, according to Bultmann, needs interpretation as judgment of the world, and as judgment and deliverance of humanity as well. The cross involves a redemptive word. All who hear it need to appropriate it by being crucified with Christ.

Concentration on the cross, however, is not enough. Cross and resurrection form a whole. Faith in the resurrection is not belief in a miracle disrupting the course of nature, but appreciation of the saving efficacy of the cross. In the kerygma, cross and resurrection go together. In the preaching of the Word of God both are means of salvation.

Julius Schniewind has already observed that in Bultmann's essay "the synoptic gospels are never so much as mentioned as evidence for the kergyma, and John figures only as the satellite of Paul."[6] Bultmann, in turn, complained about Schniewind's metaphorical view that Jesus Christ "incorporates his own in himself as a king includes his people."[7] The debate on demythologizing might have taken on a different character had these reflections been pressed further. Even Bultmann saw Jesus' destiny bound up with that of the whole human race.[8] But the issue of the corporateness of selfhood was not seen as central at that time. Bultmann was still caught up in the centrality of the Enlightenment struggle of "God the Problem."[9] In this orientation his primary concern was whether or not God could act in the "modern world" of cause and effect. He wanted to stress our being addressed by God here and now — being questioned and judged by him.[10] And yet he never took the person of Jesus into account in this regard. Jesus' struggle in Israel made little difference.

It is almost painful at times to listen to the individualistic emphasis of Bultmann's thought. At stake in the preaching of the word are "my existential self-understanding, . . . my concrete encounter, my past and future."[11] The presupposition seems to be all along that the self involved in the self-understanding presents no real problem. God somehow has to prove to the self that God can act in the world. But the possibility that the self might be asking the wrong questions on this score hardly enters the picture.

In Bultmann's interpretation we are struggling with the Christian view of the cross as a saving event. We are very much on the "Christian" side of the Jesus story. If one also takes into account the existentialist mold into which Bultmann was wont to press this event one becomes sensitive to the possibility of an ideology operative here that might conceal the more radical dimensions of the Gospels.

I can no longer simply begin with the assumption that God always acts in Christian origins the same way with cross and resurrection as hermeneutical norm. The cards are being stacked too neatly by the accustomed western interpretations of God's action. Before I answer the question whether God is acting in history I first need to ask: *Which* action are we talking about? The notion that God is acting in history dare not become a matter of course. With Bultmann in any case it is tied too quickly into the cross and the resurrection theme alone.

With Barth it is in principle very much the same, his differences with Bultmann in detail notwithstanding. In fact, here we have a much more confident affirmation of God acting in history. Revelation is assumed to be taking place all along in the Covenant story. In the cross, the Judge finally takes the place of the judged and lets them go free. In the Resurrection this becomes manifest as truth. "If it is the case that Jesus Christ has made our sin His own, then He stands in our place as the Representative of our evil case and it is He who answers for it (as ours). It is then (as ours) the sin which is forgiven us in Him. . . . Made sin for us, He stands in our place."[12] As the story of Barth's dogmatics unfolds it becomes clear that Barth accepts the picture language of the New Testament as a whole. The *Church Dogmatics* is one vast effort of faithfulness to the scriptural witness. On its own grounds, this move makes sense. That is, if one agrees to the principle one can also agree to most of what is being proposed in detail.

Somehow in Barth the premise is also the result. Jesus Christ becomes the true history not only of humankind, but also of God. And it needs especially to be underlined that Jesus' history is for Barth our history: "We have been speaking of Him and therefore

of justified man, of His history and therefore our own."[13] For
Barth, this is not a merely symbolical or metaphorical way of
speaking: it is the direct ontological truth of history.[14] It involves
in more ways than one a great difference from Bultmann. Barth
acknowledges a real role of the person of Jesus. And yet Jesus as
person, in the end, is subject to the cross-resurrection theme, so
that the primary focus of Barth's doctrines of incarnation and
atonement is the transaction between God and humankind: God's
righteousness is restored, God's justice prevails, God's grace
triumphs, and humanity is again acceptable in God's sight.

The genuine strength of Barth's paradigm cannot be denied.
In contradistinction to Bultmann, Barth lets cross and resurrection interact significantly with the person of Jesus. What is more,
Barth carefully emphasizes "the one covenant"[15] that binds Jew
and Gentile together. It is only that Barth does not raise the issue
of Jesus' personhood within Israel on its own merit. So here too
the power conflict between the rabble and the powerful is overlooked *as a significant factor of theological construction.*

The point we need to keep in mind is that the western paradigm
of Christology largely sees the Jesus story as a transaction between
God and humankind: God is satisfied, and all is well with my soul.
The implications of the new human selfhood initiated in the
person of Jesus do not become a factor decisive for theological
reflection.[16] This may seem for many an irrelevant point. But it
may well be that the tradition has so "brainwashed" us that we
tune out significant data from the beginning of theological research.

## JESUS AS JEW

One should not get the impression that there have been new
data "unearthed" in the Jesus story that now need to be evaluated.
It is mainly a question of what we do with data already available.
Geza Vermes, in *Jesus the Jew,* offers some plain points that delimit
the blindspot of systematic theology fairly well. There is first of all
the contrast between Galilee, the countryside Jesus came from,
and Judea. In one way it is the contrast between rural life and the
metropolis: "At home among the simple people of rural Galilee,

he must have felt quite alien in Jerusalem."[17] Jesus came from among those not belonging to the Jerusalem power structure. He was not a member of an in-group: "It appears that in the eyes of the authorities, whether Herodian or Roman, any person with a popular following in the Galilean tetrarchy was at least a potential rebel."

Some Jewish leaders apparently felt on edge: "It would seem in effect that during a period of riots in Jerusalem the unspecified charge leveled against Jesus by the civic leaders was that as a teacher he had won over many Jews." So it is understandable "that the first Jewish Galilean version of Jesus' life and teaching was conceived in a politico-religious spirit." The Galileans on the whole were considered peasants who carried the stigma "of a religiously uneducated person." The long and short of it is that Jesus usurped the prerogative of power. Did a Galilean have the right to teach the people? "Jesus became a political suspect in the eyes of the rulers of Jerusalem because he was a Galilean."

Obviously Jesus and his disciples, while breaking new faith ground in Galilee, were not working on a textbook of systematic theology.What we first find in Jesus' words and acts are new shades of meaning, slight shifts of emphasis, and new relationships between human beings. And yet in a placid countryside and in the midst of a quiet community a powerful nuclear fission of the spirit takes place. A new dynamics enters the historical process. The rabble claimed its rightful place as daughters and sons before God against the tutelage of the religious professionals. Power was redistributed. It reached even the most wretched and debased. What was happening was not necessarily something absolutely unique to Jesus: "Jesus and the Essenes thought that the social outcasts and oppressed would become the first in the very near divine future."[18] Yet in the person of Jesus what was common to him and other Jews became effectively embodied in lasting relationships in public space. In Jesus the new power distribution found the momentum to persevere *in history*.

We are not adducing new material, but lifting out what is often overlooked. The God of Abraham, Isaac, and Jacob was struggled with in Galilee in a new politico-religious constellation. God was no longer cooped up in the Jerusalem temple under the sovereign control of the priest and the rulers. God proved sovereign again in the struggle of the people who sought their destiny in the person of Jesus.

What we have here is also a struggle between new and old categories of understanding (cf. Matt. 9:17). Nothing is put neatly in small pieces on a platter of understanding. The crucial factor remains the conflict, the striving, the new dynamics. Later on St. Paul will talk about "God in Christ." But this is not a neat formula either. One always has to see it within a justice context.

"God in Christ" is first of all a missionary formula that makes the God of Abraham, Isaac, and Jacob for me as a Gentile my very own, always within the context of the basic power conflict. Here in the person of Jesus a *power shift* begins. While the immediate consequences were not "worldwide," the process of history was infused with a new change agent effecting a new direction and a new quality of life. The result was a new power balance, a new justice.

Eugene B. Borowitz, in his paper "Contemporary Christologies: A Jewish Response,"[19] offers us an excellent point of entry for new reflection. He believes that with an approach like Barth's no dialogue is possible between Jews and Christians. There is no common ground in a mutually accepted interpretation of Scripture. A dialogue might be possible, however, at the point where the power shift in Israel is seen by Jew and Christian alike and where both can ponder the effect of the outcast's central place in God's work. The battle between traditionalists and liberals that Borowitz sees as central might be transcended at this point.

Borowitz argues the christological issues with a great number of contemporary theologians. Our brief summary of his critique merely seeks to show the lacuna in Christian theology which in part may account for the lack of encounter between Jewish thought and systematic theology. The critique points to a reconsideration of material in the Gospel story too long neglected by the systematic theologian.

A core objection by Borowitz pertains to overemphasis on individualism. Jesus seems to function only in terms of a personal paradigm. He is the center of the Christian life. Jewish life is centered in the people's history and offers a more social context for individual existence. The question is how Christians can move from an individual as central cult figure to a sense of social responsibility. Other issues arise in regard to the irreplaceability of the individual, the reconciliation of humanity with God, and the capacity to love an invisible God. Time and again the Christian emphasis on the uniqueness of Jesus seems to obscure God's transcendence through its identification with contingency. Even the Christ on the cross theme obscures this transcendence: powerlessness as such does not clarify the reality of God, whereas holiness does.

I am much indebted to the Borowitz analysis. But I am not going to suggest that Christian theologians now dissociate themselves from the superstructure of Christian belief that has accumulated over nearly two thousand years of church history. It is our heritage, and I, for one, intend to stand by it.[20] But it cannot be denied that in many ways the superstructure has also thoroughly obfuscated the pristine power of the originative Christian event. Would it be possible for Jews and Christians to dialogue on Jesus as a Jew not yet caught up in Christian individualism? Would it perhaps be possible for Christians to see how he embodied the corporateness of Jewish selfhood in a new way so that the outcast and oppressed were also acknowledged as part of the self? And might it not be already at this point that a new act of God changed the human condition so radically that the memory of this act never got lost? If there is any point for the Christian to talk about God's incarnation, it has something to do with Jesus' Jewishness. To stay with the Christian formula, God did not become merely man, he became a Jew.

The question, of course, is what this could possibly mean. It amounts to much more than a merely academic argument. The search for global human community is taxing us all. Books are written, groups gather for study, and foundations publish reports. Time and again these various efforts come down to the question of the character of human selfhood. A recent Hazen Foundation study puts it in concise terms: "This concern for the other, this transcendence of self, whether that 'self' be an individual, nation, class, race or creed, is, we venture to affirm, the essence of morality. Without such morality, not only will the human condition remain highly precarious, but the needed universalism, even if achieved, will prove to be impotent and without content and the desired humanism will bring more evil than good."[21] Both the Jewish and the Christian community need to ask: Is transcendence of self indeed the essence of morality? Is "morality" all we have to be concerned about? What does our common tradition have to contribute? Could not the feeling of the need to transcend the self be exactly the problem? Was Jesus as Jew perhaps saying that the self is dual or corporate in the first place and need not be transcended, but merely calls for acknowledgment in its true structure?

Might it not be that only in a false arrangement of power we feel the need to "transcend" the self? It may well be that the self offers the appearance of separateness where human beings begin to lord it over one another, that is, where power is abused to divide humankind into persons and non-persons. In order to make a clear point here the Christian needs the Jewish understanding of Jesus' selfhood. This does not mean that this will immediately solve all problems. But there might just be a fighting chance that we finally will find a common ground of Scripture interpretation that helps "the needed universalism"[22] to emerge creatively. Christianity alone seems incapable of making the contribution humankind so sorely needs today. Within our western tradition it will take a concerted effort of seeking to recover our common roots.

The interdependence of the notion of selfhood with the issue of power is the crucial point. The Hazen report immediately speaks of "the differential in power that exists between nations and cultures." In regard to reconstituting the human community "one of the questions to bear in mind is how to overcome, limit or compensate for the distortions and limitations imposed by the power configurations among nations."[23]

To some it might seem that this still leaves us entirely in the realm of *Realpolitik* (not pertinent to theology). But this would be a misunderstanding of the interdependence of theology and culture: "The flow of culture is often a function of the differentials in power, of political and economic strength, but it can only be maintained if the stronger power is culturally productive as well."[24] Theology needs to understand that the exercise of power is a function of one's view of selfhood. As long as the self is able to bracket segments of humanity as not part of the self the power differential will wreak havoc on some members of the human family.

In the prevailing notion of selfhood in western culture, we usually have value as human beings when in some form we acquire power over others. We think of making it up the ladder of success — one way of acquiring power over others. One glorious little self is still pitted against another not so glorious self. The resources of Israel can be marshalled against this outlook at the point where Jesus as member of Israel created the power balance between human beings by acknowledging the marginals as part of the self. Power corrupts at the point where the weak, the poor, and the maimed are viewed as non-persons. And absolute power corrupts absolutely where everyone else is viewed as nonexistent except as foil for one's self-aggrandizement.

## THEOLOGY IN RED, WHITE, AND BLACK—AND ISRAEL

It is on this background that we need to look once more at the ethnic struggle Protestant theology went through this past decade. To some it seemed an exercise in futility. And yet, in the end, this was the only way we were able to recover the corporate truth of the Christian faith that had escaped us for so long. It was an overpowering acknowledgment of corporate selfhood that in New Testament times finally brought Jew and Gentile together in one humanity. Here the wall of enmity had been broken down.

Benjamin Reist offers us an excellent overview of what ethnic struggles have been all about theologically.[25] In the creative development of a position of his own, Reist puts the fundamental issues before us once more. In a few strokes he makes it clear from the outset why theology can no longer disregard the colorline.

I will try to draw out Reist's basic point and will then seek to extend his approach along the line indicated in my argument. It should be clear throughout, however, that for Christianity the need of overcoming our separations does not lie in the awareness of our pluralism as such. It lies in the originative event, not because of its primitiveness, but because of its ontological truth. In Jesus as a Jew the true structure of human selfhood was acknowledged.

How can we best get at the root hermeneutical issue? Reist begins with an analysis of the historical experience of American theology: "We hear much talk these days of an American theology. None worthy of the name will ever emerge unless it has its beginnings as a theology in red, white, and black."[26] It is a matter of course to Reist that there is more to humanity than these three colors:

> These are not all the hues that make up the full mosaic that is humanity. The attempt is beginning only, envisioning the unfolding one day of theology in red, white, black, brown, and yellow, against the background of the blue earth, our mother. But the process must begin with the attempt at a theology in red, white, and black. For these are the historic American components of that full mosaic that is humanity, all of which is now present in this land. These are the three components that initially became indigenous by way of a tragically brutal but nevertheless irreversible process.[27]

It cannot be denied that it was within this context that the ethnic challenge impacted theology. But we dare not overlook how much the Cartesian starting point of theology may still remain with us unless with forethought we exclude it from our premises. Are we going to define American theology as theology in red, white, and black right away at its beginnings or are we going to ground its beginnings in the originative event? Theology in red, white, and black can still appear as basing true selfhood on human experience. And so again, in the end, God-certainty might come as an afterthought based on our experience. In Christian origins it is first of all the sovereign God who empowers human beings to acknowledge the structure of selfhood.

Express acknowledgment of "the gospel of Jesus the Christ that is at the heart of the being of all the churches"[28] comes only after Reist's significant reflections on red, white, and black have already placed us in our American context. A little while later Reist quotes Vincent Harding: "There will be no new beginnings for a nation that refuses to acknowledge its real past."[29] By the same token, one could say, there will be no new beginnings for a *church* that refuses to acknowledge its real past. Reist certainly does not wish to get caught in not acknowledging the past. In the end of the book he relates to the originative events of the church as forcefully as one might ever hope. But can we afford not to do this relating right at the beginning? Does not God's liberation hinge on what God has done once and for all in the person of Jesus, so that we need to be incorporated into his selfhood *before* we try to weld together red, white, and black?

There still is a very fundamental issue at stake in our struggle with the ethnic dimensions of our American existence. The point of our identification with black or red today (becoming black or becoming red) is not a general overcoming of the color-line, but a specific overcoming of the oppression-line. The color-line alone is not the problem. It makes for a dilemma because it is used as opportunity for one person to lord it over another, debasing the other. Speaking of becoming black or becoming red[30] is a new attempt to find a contemporary mode for grasping Jesus' radical identification with oppression.

This is the factor that our focus on Jesus as Jew keeps inescapably before us. The small beginnings of Christianity in Judaism contain the reconstitution of human selfhood exactly at the point where the individual self is usurping the power of the corporate self. It is not built into the created structure of human selfhood that one individual should lord it over another. No human being has a right to prey on the other: "Even the possums and the skunks know better! Even the weasels and the meadow mice have a natural regard for their own blood and kin. Only the insects are low enough to do the low things people do — like those ants that swarm on poplars in the summertime, greedily husbanding little green aphids for the honeydew they secrete."[31] It is their corruption of power that enables human beings to prey on each other. Underlying the power corruption is the exclusion of the other from one's selfhood. The Jesus event acknowledges the other as part of the self, especially the marginal other. The commandment to love the other as oneself is not an invitation to love an alien other, but finally to discover the other as co-constitutive of one's self. This awareness of one's identity in corporate selfhood emerges in the church in the wrestle with the Jesus event at the ground level of Christian origins in Judaism.

Unless we see that our struggle with theology in red, white, and black has this ethnic bottom-line in Judaism we bypass the basic "ethnic dilemma" of Christianity. It is Christian identity in Jesus that we are time and again unclear about. And this means, that we are unclear about Christian identity in the corporate selfhood of Israel.[32] In Jesus' corporate selfhood we become incorporated into a power balance that makes us different human beings. It was in the struggle for this power balance that in Judea the powers that be decided against justice. But the power issue was not peculiar to Israel: "You know that the rulers of the Gentiles lord it over them, and their great men exercise authority over them. It shall not be so among you; but whosoever would be great among you must be your servant" (Matt. 20:25f.). This does not mean that Jesus was trying to turn people into lackeys of the powerful. He stressed mutuality in the corporate self where there is equality because of mutual acknowledgment of justice. This *reconstitution of power* is seldom considered very important, although the cross followed from it.

## BECOMING VULNERABLE

It is impossible from the Christian perspective to speak of Jesus as though his cause were a matter of sheer humanism. In his power struggle God's power is at stake. The fulfillment of the great and first commandment is interdependent with the second in that God's presence is involved in the human being. Jesus sought to free human beings for an adequate imaging of God in balancing power. In the process, God also proved to be deeply immersed in this effort. God appeared as the power that undoes the human corruption of power. The only way human corruption knew to assert itself was the attempt to destroy the new balance of power. Thus the Cross. And then the Resurrection. New problems emerge here. But everything goes wrong if we pontificate about the presence of God in Jesus without taking the Jewish context into account.[33] All along the first Jews who witnessed to the cross did not mean to suggest that now the power balance had disappeared in sheer powerlessness. Tremendous strength had been sustained even in the cross. The cross had occurred basically in terms of: "My power is made perfect in weakness" (2 Cor. 12:8). It says that power is perfected, not that it turns into sheer powerlessness.

We cannot go on here without recalling Auschwitz. Any Christian theology that does not know modesty at this point has hardly understood the character of corporate selfhood. Emil L. Fackenheim has brought this out with great clarity:

> A good Christian suggests that perhaps Auschwitz was a divine reminder of the sufferings of Christ. Should we not ask instead whether his Master himself, had He been present at Auschwitz, could have resisted degradation and dehumanization? What are the sufferings of the Cross compared to those of a mother whose child is slaughtered to the sound of laughter or the strains of a Viennese waltz? This question may sound sacrilegious to Christian ears. Yet we dare not shirk it, for we — Christian as well as Jew — must ask: at Auschwitz, did the grave win the victory after all, or, worse than the grave, did the devil himself win?[34]

Fackenheim's point about the difference between Jesus' sufferings and Auschwitz needs to be accepted as premise of any solidarity. Fackenheim effectively punctures the tendency among Christians to make the cross the acme of human suffering.

Jesus' cross became the occasion for a number of Jews, the early apostles and their followers, to understand their existence in a life-affirming way. The cross, in the light of the resurrection, was viewed as sustaining corporate selfhood through and beyond death. Here some of the promises to Israel seem fulfilled: Gentiles were drawn into the Covenant.

All my theological tasks as a Gentile hinge on the fact that my notion of God is rooted in Israel's God. Whatever I do to clarify my notion of God is an attempt to clarify Israel's notion of God as communicated to me through the first Jews who were Jesus' followers. I do not wish to distort the Jewish notion of God. But at the root of my Gentile faith in God lies a reconstituted Jewish notion of God. I do not have to decide to become vulnerable at this point.[35] I am vulnerable. The problem is that I cannot "prove" the involvement of this God as countervailing force in the power struggle of history. Christianity itself has certainly not lived up to God's involvement in history in any convincing way.

Auschwitz seems utterly to contradict God's presence in history. Emphasis on the powerlessness of God is certainly not the answer. Instead, there is the immensity of evil to be considered. The human potential for conspiracy in evil seems limitless. People do rise up and play God. Power corrupts. Arrogation of absolute power corrupts absolutely. This also became the Christian sin. The Holocaust is an occurrence for which a Christianized people, the German people, became accountable in terms of a demonic usurpation of power.

Jesus' cross is the exact opposite, a sacrifice of life to end all human sacrifice, the countering of usurped power by a power balance.[36] From Jesus' corporate selfhood, interdependent with Cross and Resurrection, power breaks forth that empowers human beings to create decent power structures. The search for God's presence in history is thus the quest not for powerlessness, but for countervailing power, affirming life and enabling people to exist as persons. Yet when Christians suggest that at the cross the mismanagement of power ceases they become utterly vulnerable. There is a credibility gap. Only a Christianity renewed in corporate selfhood might bridge it.[37]

## CHRISTOLOGY AFTER AUSCHWITZ

What are some of the practical implications of the preceding systematic theology argument about the significance of Jesus? One implication is a sharper focus in the Jewish/Christian dialogue. Michael B. McGarry has given us a thoughtful summary of the issues in *Christology after Auschwitz*. Here we see immediately what is questioned most in the recent dialogue, namely, the unique place and universal significance of Jesus as Messiah, "absolute finality in Jesus as the only way to God."[38] The early church is viewed as at least anti-Judaic, with its anti-Judaism bias providing the basis for the sad history of Christian anti-Semitism. In other words, primitive Christianity is not free of an ideological stance we willy-nilly appropriate if we appeal uncritically to the authority of the New Testament Scriptures as foundation of the theology of the church.

It is only too clear that the church throughout its history has made tragic blunders, has at times called Jews God-killers, and has pitted Christians against Jews. What anti-Semitism has done in history is much more than a shameful page of western civilization. It happened mainly because theory was put first, theory about the ultimacy or universality of Christ. The end was the horror of the Holocaust.

On the premise of the preceding argument anti-Semitism is not primarily due to some strange anti-Judaism of the New Testament, but develops on a false hermeneutical premise of later Christian theology. Theory about the Christ comes first. Only then can one be a Christian.

What the New Testament is saying is very plain: Messiah Jesus is God's self-realization in history in one person (incarnation). The event is not meant to show preference for "Christians" and rejection of Jews or Hindus. No person before God is just, not one.

The hermeneutic of this event cannot initially be grafted on theory. As little as this point may seem to yield, it is the crucial starting point for Christian theology. Praxis comes first, Jesus' praxis.

The time of pure Christology theory has come to an end. Christ's coming was not about theory, but about praxis. Christ is meaningless apart from his praxis of identification with the oppressed.

There are a few understandings we need to draw from this datum. (1) The covenant of God with Israel has not been superseded. Otherwise the Law and the Prophets would not be part of our Bible. Keeping the books of Israel in the church, we acknowledge that God still acts through the witnesses of God among Israel. (2) The God of Israel through Messiah Jesus acts

among the Gentiles as well. It is the same God who acts in both
Israel and the church. What we have in Jesus is God embodied,
and that means embodied in Israel. But that does not mean that
God does not act among the Hindus, for example. (3) What the
words of the New Testament want to communicate is not superior
concepts or pictures, but power. "The kingdom of God does not
consist in words, but in power" (1 Cor. 4:20).

For the present discussion between Christians and Jews related
in the McGarry book there are two major camps in regard to
Judaism and Christianity: Christologies of discontinuity, and
Christologies of continuity.

The basic premise of the preceding argument is at odds with
the Christologies of discontinuity, a position that aims at the
conversion of the Jews to Christianity. Judaism here has no right
to exist other than as preparation for Christianity.[39] Jews are a
people who do not yet believe in Jesus Christ. There is no positive
significance in the continued existence of the Jews and no room
for any Jewish witness to contemporary salvation. The Christian
church is the sole eschatological reality.[40] The Jews are viewed as
blind to their own Scriptures. If they were able to see they would
also regard Jesus as the perfect fulfillment of Old Testament
messianic prophecies.[41]

The Christologies of continuity fall into a number of approaches. Some hold that in the Old Testament there already is a
two-covenant reality. There is the covenant with Israel as a whole,
and then there is the covenant with David and the house of David.
It is difficult to grasp all the implications of the intricate argument. The main point in the McGarry book seems to stress that
God covenants not only with a people, but also with the individual. So the Old and New Testaments are not two chronologi-
cally related covenants in sequence. There is already an "overlap-
ping" of covenants in the Old Testament. One way of seeing the
relevance of the argument is to claim that Jews and Christians are
"equal, complementary partners in bringing mankind to the messianic age, each making his own proper contribution based on the
revelation from which each respectively springs."[42] The Jews
witness to messianic fulfillment in terms of the mission of the
covenant people, the Christians in terms of the *missio Dei* through
Christ bringing the messianic age. The sum of it can also be put

somewhat differently: "Whereas in Israel the Covenant of David is made subservient to the Covenant of the Confederacy, in Christianity the opposite is the case."[43]

According to McGarry, there is also another way to state very much the same thing. The church cannot be satisfied with a Logos-Christology that presents Jews simply as anonymous Christians. "Jesus is Christ in the fullest sense only at the end of time. Jesus was Messiah in a proleptic, anticipatory way; Jesus brings the grace that makes humanity yearn for fulfillment. . . . The sentence that Jesus is the Christ will be true in the fullest sense only at the end of time."[44] The difficulty with this position is that it subordinates Christology to a kind of utopian thinking in which God has no *topos* as yet.

Many assume that Logos-Christology makes Christians the real thing and Jews only an epiphenomenon, anonymous Christians. Yet the whole point of New Testament Logos-Christology is not to make Jews anonymous Christians, but to make Christians adopted Jews: "If some of the branches were broken off, and you, a wild olive shoot, were grafted in their place to share the richness of the olive tree, do not boast over the branches" (Rom. 11:17).

Before a few final critical observations we need to take a look at one more Christology of continuity mentioned by McGarry. There is the paradox of Christology, Jesus continuing to be the Christ, the bringer of messianic gifts. Yet his actual role is viewed in terms of functions pre- or non-messianic: "Jesus is *not yet* the Christ."[45] Resurrection and Christ-experience function in a paradigmatic way for Christians, the way the Exodus functions as foundation for hope among Jews. Neither invalidates the other! Each simply speaks to a different group of people.[46] Christ is mainly a paradigm of hoping, while traditional Christology has claimed an efficacious salvation through Jesus' life.

In the Christologies of continuity the first position seems to retain the core of Christology, the second orients it toward the future, and the third abrogates it in principle.

As much as we sympathize with the new Christologies as they struggle over a sane relationship between Israel and the church, and as much as we want to acknowledge the significant vistas they have opened up, it is difficult to agree with the terms in which they have been framed. They are still largely beholden to the old hermeneutic, where thought rises from thought, theory from theory. According to the old hermeneutic, the Bible has to deliver the concepts of the Pantokrator, the Son of God, sitting on high at the right hand of God, true God and true man. Today the metaphysical has largely been transferred to the eschatological. But the bone of contention is still theory—in terms of Jesus as the fulfillment of messianic hopes now, or in the future messianic age, or as merely the paradigm of hope.

What is not touched upon in the debate covered in the McGarry book is the hermeneutical starting point of theology. Any hermeneutic that begins with abstract theory cannot help arguing abstractly over whether Jesus is the one who is to come or whether we should look for another. All Jesus is reported to have said in response to messianic speculations was: "Go tell John what you hear and see: the blind receive their sight and the lame walk, lepers are cleansed and the deaf hear, and the dead are raised up, and the poor have good news preached to them. And blessed is he who takes no offense at me" (Matt. 11:4ff.).

What happened in Jesus was that a hermeneutic of Christology was turned into a hermeneutic of Christopraxis. We need to explain to the church that in this praxis God entered history, so that thought finally could rise from praxis and we too could act our way into thinking.

It is a peculiar kind of praxis. The church before long missed the point. The church always does — easily.

Whether for Jews or Gentiles, the issue of Jesus becomes whether God is on the side of the losers or mainly on the side of the powers that be, the status quo, spiritual beauty culture, and the ecclesiastical establishment. The mandate of justice is overriding: "Seek first the kingdom of God and God's justice, and all other things shall be added to you" (Matt. 6:33).

The church as ecclesiastical establishment soon began to cover up the battle of God among the oppressed, very much like the ecclesiastical establishment in Judaism had covered up the truth in Jesus' day. The metaphysical obscurantism of Christianity has long been proved inappropriate by reasonable women and men. But the eschatological obscurantism of messianic theory overriding praxis has yet to be proved futile.

What then will be left? Jesus as moral example only? Most

certainly not. What we have is the spiritual power of metaphorical language creating intermediate structures for overcoming injustice, pain, and meaninglessness. Metaphors begin to form the body of Christ, the church, which makes sense in terms of the new corporate selfhood Jesus introduces, identifying with nonpersons, the lost, the rejected.

So what is praxis hermeneutic? It is taking the metaphorical language of the New Testament as praxis-event that introduces Christopraxis into humankind. Christians engaged in this praxis have more in common with Jews also involved in Christopraxis than with fellow Christians not so involved. It does not take Jesus to get Jews involved in Christopraxis. One only has to remember Isaiah 53. It takes Jesus for God's self-realization in history to occur, so that the Gentiles be included. The sacraments celebrated by the Christian community concretize God's self-realization beyond Israel.

The emphasis on metaphorical language gives up the priority of concept and symbol in Christian theology. So finally, in terms of method, we are able again to understand God. Faith seeking understanding makes sense now in terms of praxis seeking justice. Faith is certainly not excluded. But it finds a new quality: "My teaching is not mine, but his who sent me; if any person's will is to do God's will, this person shall know whether the teaching is from God or whether I am speaking on my own authority" (John 7:16f.).

Christology is subject to Christopraxis. It seems a possibility for Jews and Christians alike. It does not make Christianity superior. It acknowledges God as superior. We are not justified because we are Christians. We make sense as humans because God makes sense of us, both Jews and Christians. God makes sense of all humans. God is the way to God. Messiah Jesus told us so.

## NOTES

1. "Whatever Happened to Theology?", *Christianity and Crisis*, 35:8 (May 12, 1975), pp. 106–20.
2. As I have put it, for example, in "Towards the Waiting God," in *The Future of Hope: Theology as Eschatology* (New York, 1970), pp. 51–71.

3. Cf. my *Liberation Theology* (New York, 1972), p. 179. From the notion of "costly love" it was only a small step to the notion of God as justice.

4. New English Bible.

5. Hans Werner Bartsch (ed.), *Kerygma and Myth* (New York, 1961), p. 35.

6. Ibid., p. 67.

7. Ibid., p. 106.

8. Ibid., p. 112.

9. Title of the book by Gordon D. Kaufman, *God the Problem* (Cambridge, 1972).

10. Bartsch, *Kerygma and Myth,* p. 196f.

11. Ibid., p. 203.

12. Karl Barth, *Church Dogmatics,* IV/1 (Edinburgh, 1956), p. 241.

13. Ibid., p. 629.

14. Ibid., p. 636.

15. Ibid., p. 670.

16. The only place I know of in Barth where this dimension breaks through adequately is IV/1, p. 106. But the insight does not begin to function significantly in this volume in Barth's further theological construction.

17. Geza Vermes, *Jesus the Jew* (London, 1973), p. 49. The following quotations are from pp. 49–57.

18. David Flusser, *Jesus* (New York, 1969), p. 77.

19. Presented at the annual meeting of the American Theological Society, April 4-5, 1975, New York.

20. Even as Barth is using the Christian dogmatic tradition for the construction of his theological perspective he is aware of its function as "defense mechanism." See IV/1, p. 127. Cf. Paul Tillich, *Systematic Theology,* II (Chicago, 1957), p. 141f.

21. *Reconstituting the Human Community,* a report sponsored by the Hazen Foundation (New Haven, 1972), p. 28.

22. Ibid.

23. Ibid., p. 10.

24. Ibid., p. 24.

25. Benjamin A. Reist, *Theology in Red, White, and Black* (Philadelphia, 1975).

26. Ibid., p. 25.

27. Ibid., p. 24f.

28. Ibid., p. 32.

29. Ibid., p. 45.

30. Ibid., p. 180.

31. William Styron, *The Confessions of Nat Turner* (New York, 1966), p. 221.

32. Recently James Wm. McClendon, Jr., *Biography as Theology* (Nashville and New York, 1974), has offered the significant suggestion of the need to develop an "ethic of character-in-community" (p. 32). Since "Christianity turns upon the character of Christ" (p. 38), it is time and again necessary to recover the dimensions of his selfhood as center of Christian character-in-community. Character is first of all perseverance of commitments in the basic structure of human selfhood. This is what Jesus brings to the fore. The new thinking that is going on right now in recovering the corporate dimensions of theological work finds strong support in the excellent essay by Leland J. White, "Christology and Corporate Ministry," *American Benedictine Review*, 26:1 (March 1975), pp. 54-74.

33. It created endless havoc in theology when Schleiermacher declared: "Christianity cannot in any wise be regarded as a remodelling or a renewal and continuation of Judaism" (*The Christian Faith* [Edinburgh, 1928], p. 61).

34. Emil L. Fackenheim, *God's Presence in History* (New York, 1972), p. 75.

35. Carol Christ in "Whatever Happened to Theology?," *Christianity and Crisis* (May 12, 1975), p. 114, speaks of being "vulnerable to experience." It may be that the most taxing vulnerability for the Christian theologian comes in the encounter with Judaism.

36. In order to explain fully what is implied one would need to offer an analysis of the Christian doctrines of the atonement, especially their assessment in the Anglo-Saxon tradition. For a convenient overview see Robert S. Paul, *The Atonement and the Sacraments* (New York, 1960), pp. 135ff. And a dialogue with more recent christological statements would be inevitable. The general tendency still is to orient oneself in the way the issues were raised in the eighteenth- and nineteenth-century European discussion. Two recent volumes offer helpful foci for orientation: Hans W. Frei, *The Identity of Jesus Christ* (Philadelphia, 1975); Eugene TeSelle, *Christ in Context* (Philadelphia, 1975). For the initial impetus of the present essay I am indebted to discussions with Brevard S. Childs and James A. Sanders.

37. The perspective here proposed has far-reaching consequences. The power balance reality in Jesus goes beyond the ethnic line to the male-female relationship. For an overview of the issues see Rosemary Radford Ruether, *Religion and Sexism* (New York, 1974).

38. Michael B. McGarry, *Christology after Auschwitz* (New York, 1977), p. 85.

39. Ibid., p. 65.
40. Ibid., p. 68.
41. Ibid., pp. 70f.
42. Ibid., p. 68.
43. Ibid., p. 81.
44. Ibid., p. 83.
45. Ibid., p. 89.
46. Ibid., p. 90.

# CHAPTER THREE

# Schleiermacher and the Problem of Power

*The first word . . . to be spoken by religion to the people of our time must be a word spoken against religion.*

—*Paul Tillich*[1]

The name Friedrich Schleiermacher appears time and again as orientation point of the modern theological endeavor. In an April 1976 *Christian Century* review of *Blessed Rage for Order* by the Roman Catholic theologian David Tracy, the reviewer, Edward Farley, found that the best way to describe Tracy's Christology was to call it basically "Schleiermacherian."[2] When shortly afterward Dean William Ferm in the same journal wrote about "Protestant Liberalism Reaffirmed," the first witness for the defense was *Friedrich Schleiermacher:*

All doctrines must be extracted from "the inward experience of Christian people," wrote Friedrich Schleiermacher, 19th century progenitor of 20th century Protestant liberalism. To be sure, this view of inward experience or feeling was more narrow and specific than one that today's liberals would espouse. Experience includes one's total life, past and present, personal and social, aesthetic and scientific, mystical and moral.[3]

Immediately two things stand out from these gleanings: (1) Schleiermacher today still serves to characterize the liberal theological stance, even that of a Roman Catholic. (2) Schleiermacher is still widely held to be the progenitor of a theological perspective that continues to have a wide following among all

Christian creeds and churches in the West. John Macquarrie characterizes the situation well when he states: "Now that the Barthian period itself is in decline, there are signs that Schleiermacher's stock may be rising once more."[4]

## SCHLEIERMACHER MYTH OR SCHLEIERMACHER FACT?

Of Schleiermacher's continuing influence there can be little doubt. The question we are facing is whether he is adequately interpreted. Part of the thesis of this chapter is that unfortunately he is not. What we largely have is a Schleiermacher myth that is due partly to inadequate reading of his work, partly to ideological premises that use Schleiermacher for perpetuating an uncritical liberal theology.

The purpose of this chapter is not to berate Schleiermacher. His place in the history of Protestant thought is secure. His crucial achievement even Karl Barth gladly acknowledged. The point is rather to show how Schleiermacher appropriated a social order we also appropriate when we take over his theology. The exercise becomes crucial at the point where Schleiermacher becomes one of the liberal theologians most responsible for rejecting the continuity between Christianity and Judaism. Endless havoc could have been avoided had this distancing not taken place.

It is impossible for the Christian message to enter the world without acculturation. This was already the case for St. Paul. But the challenge is always to decide whether a particular acculturation is in keeping with the Gospel or whether it misrepresents and distorts it.

Part of the difficulty of adequately assessing Schleiermacher in this regard depends on the angle of vision from which he is usually viewed. He is considered one of the most progressive theologians to integrate Christian dogmatics into the modern worldview. The three-story universe of medieval and orthodox dogmatics is replaced by the infinite universe without angels, virgin births, and resurrections. The vested interest of modern science in a rational world order is here taken for Gospel for the first time in Protestant thought in any radical sense. In this regard, Schleiermacher shares in "world-construction, i.e., the processes whereby a new world is brought into being and seeks to establish itself in competition with numerous other worlds."[5] Nevertheless, for him this goes along with *"world-maintenance*, i.e., the processes whereby a given social world is maintained and legitimated for those who inhabit it."[6] Here lies the major problem for us today. In terms of world-construction Schleiermacher dwells in a halfway house, as it were. While seeming progressive in regard to science, in some respects he stays very much within the old world of social privilege determining the function of religion. Today we face a much more radical task of world-construction that does not stop at integrating merely the interests of science into the church.

The more one probes the Schleiermacher corpus the more one realizes that in spite of all the progressive features of his thought the new worldview he promotes is also the mainstay of the given social world of his day—and partly an attempt to legitimate it. Of course, there is no point arguing with history. Whatever happened has happened. But it is unfortunate that Schleiermacher's scientific progressivism covers up his limited social outlook. It is especially here that his perspective becomes a chain around our neck. He could congratulate himself for belonging to the civilized peoples and disregard the hermeneutical significance of the non-civilized of the world. Discussing the prophetic office of Christ with its attendant miracles and wondering whether the ministers of today need to produce similar signs he proclaims: "Even if it cannot be strictly proved that the Church's power of working miracles has died out (and this the Roman Church denies), yet in general it is undeniable that, in view of the great advantage in power and civilization which the Christian peoples possess over the non-Christian, almost without exception, the preachers of today do not need such signs."[7] Here Schleiermacher argues the validity of a theological point in terms of the socioeconomic and sociopolitical superiority of so-called Christian nations over inferior peoples. There are the civilized and the non-civilized. The social system simply exists. Schleiermacher's theology derives its value system mainly from what *is*.

Dean William Ferm operates with the convenient Schleiermacher myth that all Christian doctrine must be extracted from the inward experience of Christian people. That keeps him from getting into the above problematic in the first place. But Schleiermacher himself had claimed from the outset of his dogmatic work that inward Christian experience had to be viewed from the perspective of what he called "ethics,"[8] that is, his phenomenology of culture, which for him in the end also includes much of the past and present, the personal and social, the aesthetic and scientific, the mystical and moral. Schleiermacher is not thinking in privatistically religious terms, but lets religion mirror the society of his day, notwithstanding his attempt to draw a sharp theoretical line between civil government and the church.

Socially aware thinkers have always seen Schleiermacher's immersion in the needs of society. Walter Rauschenbusch observed: "The constructive genius of Schleiermacher worked out solidaristic conceptions of Christianity which were far ahead of his time."[9] But today we have to ask whether in these solidaristic conceptions Schleiermacher did not remain too much bound to his class perspective. At another point Rauschenbusch speaks of "the professional theologians of Europe, who all belong by kinship and sympathy to the bourgeois classes and are constitutionally incapacitated for understanding any revolutionary ideas, past or present."[10] One wonders whether Rauschenbusch ever examined Schleiermacher's solidaristic conceptions of Christianity from this perspective. There are at least two kinds of solidarity. *There is the solidarity of the powerful in-group that controls civilization. And there is a solidarity that includes the powerless, the voiceless poor.*

A new assessment of the progenitor of theological liberalism with regard to this simple difference in solidarity will make us better understand our heritage of Protestant thought. Schleiermacher has to be looked at from the critical perspective that non-theologians have been trying to commend to the church for a long time. Says historian Herbert J. Muller: "Christians have yet to learn the plainest lesson of history, that the churches have always consecrated some particular temporal order or ideology, in effect committed themselves to idolatry, in order to support their worldly interests. As medieval Catholicism blessed the feudal order, so Protestantism came to bless the bourgeois order, likewise without a serious sustained effort to judge or transform it."[11]

## POWER—SPIRITUAL AND SECULAR

The problem of power crystallizes the way Schleiermacher is beholden to his social context. It immediately invokes the crucial relationship between church and world. The most characteristic aspect of Schleiermacher's view of the church is that it occupies a completely spiritual sphere. It has to, because it is a modification of religion, which is in a realm all by itself for Schleiermacher. The church exists alongside the world. But its sphere is entirely different from that of the world. This goes so far that Schleiermacher makes a sharp distinction between the influence of God, the Father, in the world (creation), and the influence of Christ, the Son, in the church (redemption).[12] The power that Christ exercises is sheer spiritual power: "For it is part alike of the purity and of the perfection of His spiritual power that sensuous motives can have no share whatever in it."[13]

It is not surprising that Schleiermacher speaks of the church (where this power rules) as of "so spiritual a society."[14] What Christ's power effects in the church hinges on the "purely spiritual lordship of His God-consciousness."[15] It becomes effective through the work of the Holy Spirit "as something inward."[16] Concretely it depends on the "great inward act of preaching."[17] This is completely in keeping with what Schleiermacher otherwise outlines as his most basic views. For example, the kingdom of God itself is real only "in virtue of its inwardness."[18] What takes place in it is "a consummation of the perfection and blessedness of Christ."[19] Both of these are realities "within the sphere of spiritual life."[20]

In ever new ways Schleiermacher analyzes the spiritual dimension of the church. Thus the Holy Spirit "is the inmost vital power of the Christian Church."[21] It is especially in public worship that one can behold the power. Its major aspects are preaching, baptism, and the Lord's Supper. Preaching is "self-communication that makes for salvation."[22] Baptism is linked to regeneration, and regeneration to sanctification. "The inner fact of regeneration does not become fully certain in time to a man's own consciousness except through his progressive sanctification."[23] All of this centers again in Christ: "For the power thus ascribed to the Church is after all traced back to Christ Himself, and the fruit of baptism is represented as being not merely the remission of sin but also living union with Christ."[24] The Lord's Supper in particular makes possible a continuing union with Christ. Schleiermacher regards it as "spiritual participation in His flesh and blood with the action of partaking in the bread and wine."[25] Key experiences of the union with Christ's spiritual power are thus regeneration and sanctification.

We need to underline once more that all this takes place within "the religious sphere"[26] as an "act of the religious consciousness."[27] In principle we can view it as "the pure bent of Christ Himself, against sin and for the dissemination of His life."[28] We cannot underscore enough the pure spirituality of the realm Schleiermacher wants to stake out when he speaks of the church.

Nonetheless it also needs stressing that Schleiermacher wants to tie Christ into history. But his valiant efforts in this regard immediately seem to self-destruct because of his overall emphasis on religion as a separate sphere apart from the world as such. At one point he speaks of the incarnation of Christ "as the beginning of the regeneration of the whole human race."[29] In this context he also claims that "the supernatural in Christ is to become natural, and the Church to take shape as a natural historical phenomenon."[30] He also finds "that Christianity must develop as a force in history, and the world as it appears in Christianity is the world as it has been seized upon and permeated by the Holy Spirit."[31] But there is practically nothing *historical* that the church can do in Schleiermacher's systematic theology. All it can do is purely spiritual. It can extend regeneration and sanctification, which means it can increase the blessedness of Christ among its members and invite non-members to its spirituality.

For Schleiermacher the church is largely a haven of bliss. Its functionaries have little else to do than to keep the wheels of regeneration and sanctification turning. Dominant is the mood of harmony,[32] though it is not all sweetness and light. While the notion of peace dominates, there are also divisions in the church, but only temporarily so.[33] The power of the Keys is necessary to discipline whoever creates division or is otherwise out of line. Excommunication is possible. But "no judgment should seek to terminate the influence of the Church on the individual who has once been received into its bosom."[34]

The idea of harmony also extends to the analogy that Schleiermacher draws between church and civil government when he speaks of the Holy Spirit as common spirit: "We mean by this exactly what we mean in any earthly system of government, namely, the common bent found in all who constitute together a moral personality, to seek the advancement of the whole."[35] Schleiermacher lived before Karl Marx. I am not suggesting that Schleiermacher should have seen what Marx saw. But it needs saying that Schleiermacher did not take note of the conflicts in society as he drew the analogy between church and civil government. Anyone who today takes over Schleiermacher's view also appropriates a *harmonious* view of society that has proved deceptive. The only inequality between human beings that actually bothers Schleiermacher is the one that a misconstrued doctrine of election holds forth.[36] So the secular power struggle that constantly creates inequality between rich and poor even in the church does not enter Schleiermacher's systematic theology. Secular power is kept apart from the church. In fact, the picture that Schleiermacher draws of secular society does not know of a power struggle, only of peaceful interdependence.

All this is not to say that Schleiermacher was blind to social tasks. No lesser critic than Karl Barth has stressed that especially the older Schleiermacher showed strong social concern: "Within the frame of an outlook which today would probably be described as that of Social Liberalism he appealed very definitely and courageously to the sense of responsibility of the upper classes towards those placed at a material disadvantage by the advance of civilization."[37] What we are struggling about today is the extent to which this perspective needs to become part and parcel of the hermeneutical premises, so that it will pervade the entire dogmatic work. It is simply a fact that Schleiermacher's doctrine of the church is untouched by his later concerns. So Barth's comments are partly misleading when he wonders whether one or two things in German history "might not perhaps have turned out differently, if the educated German public, and if, for example, Schleiermacher's candidate for confirmation, Otto von Bismarck, had really heard and taken to heart what Schleiermacher evidently wished to say upon this subject."[38] In such matters of utmost dogmatic consequence it is insufficient to express good will and Christian charitableness. It becomes a *conditio sine qua non* to start the theological endeavor with an awareness of the gap between the privileged and underprivileged. To repeat the point of Herbert J. Muller, it takes a sustained effort to judge or transform the bourgeois order. That effort certainly was not part of Schleiermacher's dogmatic work.

## SCHLEIERMACHER'S GOD—THE ABSOLUTE CAUSE

We have presented only a small "sliver" from the vast Schleiermacher corpus in order to make a few basic points. (1) Schleiermacher appropriated a vision of society as a largely harmonious entity. Applying it to his theology, the resulting acculturation of the Christian faith often became surrender. (2) It was not so much that Schleiermacher made the church a purely inward reality as that he turned it into the spiritual sector of society. (3) Schleiermacher did not let the power struggle interfere with his vision of peace—"peace regarding all this abundance."[39]

It is not shameful that Schleiermacher did not see what we see today. But it is embarrassing when theologians today expect us to assent to his basic view of Christianity and the church when so much has interfered since. For us today, the mandate of the voiceless poor means that we give them a voice in our very hermeneutical presuppositions. Throughout his work Schleiermacher remained beholden to the "cultured despisers" of religion. Karl Barth, in one terse sentence, reminds us of the fact: "Paragraphs 1-31 of the *Doctrine of Faith* are written in precisely the same sense as the theological work of his youth, the *Address on Religion*."[40] So in the end it is nothing but religiosity or piety that counts. The uncultured classes did not influence his presuppositions. Christ's cross is a religious feat, as it were, totally outside the hard core of history. As far as the involvement of the church in history is concerned, Schleiermacher does not want to have much to do with the "bodily side of the matter."[41]

That the cross of Christ outside the city wall was an entrance of God into history—the likes of which has not been found elsewhere in religion—was something Schleiermacher did not consider. The sphere of history was not the place of Christ's continuing action. There is thus no notion that God in Christ is struggling with the marginals for justice and righteousness. There is only one instance where a slight preparatory step seems to have been taken in this direction: "Everything as a whole was only so determined, because, and in so far as, Christ was determined in a certain way."[42] Schleiermacher wants to say here that somehow Christ's work does influence God's work. But the thought of Christ's influence on God's own work in the world comes too late to do much good. Schleiermacher earlier had already announced his "assumption that all belonging to the human race are eventually taken up into living fellowship with Christ."[43] So in history itself not much Christ involvement takes place. God grimly carries on the cause and effect processes. The salvation of all is a future event.

The divine government of the world is going on apart from what happens in the church through Christ. So there is a perfect split in the divine reality. It runs on two tracks, as it were: part of its action goes on in the world, part of it in the church. But ne'er the twain meet. God the Father governs the world as absolute cause. In the church only spiritual things take place, dependent on Christ.

We do not mean to exclude the "cultured despisers." But they are an elite minority. Once one sees Jesus Christ taking sides with the voiceless poor, the cross is the crucible of understanding God's identification with their struggle for justice. Here the preaching of the Word appears to be the continuation of God's identification with the bloody turmoil of history. In baptism a person dies to pure spirituality as much as to pure flesh, and rises to participation in the historical struggle. The Lord's Supper deepens the participation in the struggle. The bifurcation of history into a bodily history and a spiritual history has been overcome.

Scheiermacher was not the first one to reintroduce this bifurcation. But he certainly got a lot of mileage out of it. One of the reasons why he was not true to Christian origins was his off-hand modern rejection of the Jewish Scriptures as pertinent for Christian faith. He had to make this kind of move because he wanted to elevate the God of personal experience, the God of modern religion, to the position of absolute authority. Kant had denied the accessibility of God on any grounds, rational or otherwise. Schleiermacher agreed to the cul-de-sac of every proof for the reality of God. But he did want to show even so that God was still accessible for the human being. The route he took, as is well-known, was that of the religious feeling or immediate self-consciousness. The God he found in himself, however, was also a God determined by the limitations modern science clamped on transcendence. All that Schleiermacher was able to rescue was the bare absolute cause, always generating the processes of nature under uniform pressure, but manifesting no personhood.

Schleiermacher had no use for the God of Abraham, Isaac, and Jacob. There was too much personhood in this God. So Schleiermacher declared that no particular relationship between Judaism and Christianity would have to be taken into account *theologically*. "Now if Christianity has the same relation to Judaism as to Heathenism, it can no more be regarded as a continuation of the former than of the latter."[44] It comes therefore as no surprise that Schleiermacher allowed that "the real meaning of the facts would be clearer if the Old Testament followed the New as an appendix."[45] There is a lot at stake here insofar as Schleiermacher's God in no sense directly confronts the modern person. Hugh Ross Mackintosh has sized up the dilemma:

> The pattern of the world is unchangeable, for in God its Source no change is possible. . . . Thus the Causality of God is presented as operating in the world as infinite, uniform and quite undeviating pressure, like that of a hydraulic apparatus, with its allotted equal weight on each square inch. Does then the reality of God make any difference in the particular case? Scarcely, if new creative preferential action on God's part is unnecessary, and therefore unreal.[46]

Today we are increasingly puzzled as to how one could have ever thought to be challenging the modern person with this kind of God. While no claim of divine participation in history as such makes sense as sheer claim, the Christian community cannot simply shrug off the specificity of the claims of its tradition. Schleiermacher did not *expressis verbis* want to do that either. But he felt that the tradition began only with the historical figure of Christ. And that was an utterly myopic perspective. The issue today is what could possibly evidence itself as the Sacred in terms of historical transcendence within Israel and the church. Behind Schleiermacher's notion of God lies an ontology of power in nature that is Greek rather than Hebrew and that refuses to face the contradictions in historical reality. This ontology does not question the modern self that determines the reality of God by its own whim or fancy. "A philosophy of power, ontology, as a fundamental philosophy which does not call into question the self, is a philosophy of injustice."[47]

Schleiermacher left out an entire dimension of the hermeneutical orientation of Christian origins. If one concentrates only on an elite minority of intellectuals the biblical word will be of interest only in some rarified segments. God-as-justice is a reality that did not seize Schleiermacher, although he had not entirely banned it from his field of vision. But he made it completely subject to his systematic scheme. Justice as moral claim had no function in absolute causality. The divine justice Schleiermacher allows "can be retributive only."[48] It has to be that way, since one can know God only to the extent that human consciousness allows divine reality to be known: "It is only through our consciousness of sin that we come to the idea of the divine justice."[49] The only real problem Schleiermacher finds worth examining is "the connection of evil with sin" in that God's justice may be seen "in the punishment of every particular offense"[50]—an idea he himself does not relish. So practically the notion of God's justice is irrelevant. Yet it is precisely the reality of the just God that the biblical tradition confronts us with. The place of the marginal people in the hermeneutical premises of theology is not a fanciful thought of a more activist generation, but a Christian mandate Schleiermacher overlooked in his systematic theology.

## A NEW INTERPRETATION OF SCHLEIERMACHER?

With a complex thinker like Schleiermacher we had better not jump to conclusions. Schleiermacher saw very well the interdependence of culture and church. He stretched every nerve to do justice to the need for the Christian faith to acculturate. We are not charging Schleiermacher with acculturation as bad per se. We are zeroing in on the *mode* of the acculturation, especially in view of recent attempts of reclaiming his method or part of his method. Says John Macquarrie: "I am suggesting that Schleiermacher may be able to . . . help toward rediscovering religion."[51] Macquarrie is quite aware of the social issue we have been focusing on. The religion he commends is corporate religion. He appeals to Richard R. Niebuhr's stress on "Schleiermacher's sense for social and historical relations."[52]

What we are concerned about in regard to Schleiermacher in the end is the mode of sociality in the acculturation of the Christian faith. Schleiermacher could hardly have been more advanced in his social thought. But exactly because his social views are time-bound it does not pay to appropriate them unwittingly along with his system as a whole. We, too, are involved in a new social world-construction, which demands that we be utterly critical of the social perspective of the early nineteenth century.

As an idealist Schleiermacher promotes "universal love of humanity."[53] But he does so within the context of aspirations of the rising middle class. A particular societal model influences the application of universal love. The study by Yorick Spiegel, *Theologie der bürgerlichen Gesellschaft: Sozialphilosophie und Glaubenslehre bei Friedrich Schleiermacher* (1968), is a work that clarifies the model Schleiermacher worked with. According to Spiegel, a number of good and not so good things stand side by side in Schleiermacher. We will single out three points to substantiate our thesis that the mode of sociality Schleiermacher worked with can no longer be ours.

1. Schleiermacher developed his basic theological mold for *The Christian Faith* in terms of the emerging society of free exchange of commodities with relative freedom and relative dependence.

There is the idea of the division of labor and a free play of social forces. The reality of God underlies the entire chain of interdependencies. Here the human spirit finds itself: "We discover ourselves to be in a nature-system of spiritual being."[54] Increase of mutual spiritual exchange was felt to be thoroughly creative and liberating.[55]

2. Not all are equal, however, in the free play of forces. There are the cultured and uncultured. The latter are to be tutored from the top down, as it were. There are those who already possess the spirit and who will gradually also penetrate and organize the masses. Under the notion of spirit Schleiermacher seeks to lead the middle class in the formation of culture. This provides the basis for a new elite.[56]

3. So a discrepancy has arisen between the social ideal and what actually happens in society. In ideal terms, middle-class society does not contain a contradiction. Equality and freedom are thought to have been realized. And yet there are the masses who do not share in the ideal reality. It is just that most intellectuals did not see it that way. They usually reduce all contradictions to the opposition between the person as phenomenon and the person as noumenon. But social reality does not respond to the fiat of the intellectuals. Also in Schleiermacher there is the tension between ideal equality and the overlooked reality of unreconciled conflict.[57]

One could elaborate the discrepancy in further detail. The result is always the same, namely that the mode of sociality in Schleiermacher allocates power to the already powerful and leaves the notion of universal love a mere notion. Schleiermacher was not as yet aware of the full consequences of his mode of sociality. But we today cannot in good faith transcribe his early nineteenth-century perception of reality to our late twentieth-century American scene. We are not claiming that Schleiermacher did not have a sense for social relations. What is being said is that already in his time his social categories were incommensurate with the total social reality of his day. *Communicating to the despisers of religion today involves listening to the uncultured and regarding their lot as the crucial orientation point of culture.*

The quality of a culture is ultimately not judged by its putting a man on the moon, but by how it relates to the least of its members. Since the first word of religion from Schleiermacher's day until today is spoken to the high and the mighty of culture, the word of religion to the people of our time now needs to be a word spoken against religion.

The social phenomenon to which we have addressed ourselves and which has not as yet been tackled by those who seek to reappropriate Schleiermacher has been carefully described by Herbert Marcuse. It is this kind of insight that needs to reorient American theological use of early nineteenth-century European Protestant thought:

> German culture is inseparable from its origin in Protestantism. There arose a realm of beauty, freedom, and morality, which was not to be shaken by external realities and struggles; it was detached from the miserable social world and anchored in the "soul" of the individual. This development is the source of a tendency widely visible in German idealism, a willingness to become reconciled to the social reality. . . . The "educated classes" isolated themselves from practical affairs and, thus rendering themselves impotent to apply their reason to the reshaping of society, fulfilled themselves in a realm of science, art, philosophy, and religion. That realm became for them the "true reality" transcending the wretchedness of existing social conditions; it was alike the refuge for truth, goodness, beauty, happiness, and, most important, for a critical temper which could not be turned into social channels. Culture was, then, essentially idealistic, occupied with the *idea* of things rather than with the things themselves. It set freedom of *thought* before freedom of *action*, morality before practical justice, and the inner life before the social life of man.[58]

## NOTES

1. Paul Tillich, *The Protestant Era* (Chicago, 1948), p. 185.
2. Edward Farley, "A Revisionist Model," *Christian Century*, 93:13 (April 14, 1976), p. 372.

3. Dean William Ferm, "Protestant Liberalism Reaffirmed," *Christian Century*, 93:15 (April 28, 1976), p. 411.

4. John Macquarrie, *Thinking about God* (New York, 1975), p. 158f.

5. John G. Gager, *Kingdom and Community: The Social World of Early Christianity* (Englewood Cliffs, 1975), p. 10.

6. Ibid.

7. Friedrich Schleiermacher, *The Christian Faith* (Edinburgh, 1928), p. 450. Referred to as CF hereafter.

8. CF, p. 5.

9. Walter Rauschenbusch, *A Theology for the Social Gospel* (New York, 1918), p. 27.

10. Ibid., p. 158. There has been very little research of the historical background of Schleiermacher's stance in this regard. One outstanding exception is Robert M. Bigler, *The Politics of German Protestantism: The Rise of the Protestant Church Elite in Prussia, 1815–1848* (Berkeley, 1972), pp. 166–71.

11. Herbert J. Muller, *Religion and Freedom in the Modern World* (Chicago, 1963), p. 116.

12. CF, p. 469.

13. CF, p. 472.

14. CF, p. 614.

15. CF, p. 473.

16. CF, p. 571f.

17. CF, p. 531.

18. CF, p. 536.

19. CF, p. 544.

20. CF, p. 557.

21. CF, p. 565.

22. CF, p. 612.

23. CF, p. 625.

24. CF, p. 626.

25. CF, p. 649.

26. CF, p. 687.

27. CF, p. 688.

28. CF, p. 678.

29. CF, p. 535.

30. CF, p. 537.

31. CF, p. 583f.

32. CF, p. 614.

33. CF, p. 685ff.

34. CF, p. 668.

35. CF, p. 562.

36. CF, p. 542ff.

37. Karl Barth, *Protestant Thought* (New York, 1969), p. 320.

38. Ibid. Much has yet to be carefully researched before we will be able to form an impression of the whole Schleiermacher. We at least have to keep in mind that within the time frame Barth refers to (in reference to the July revolution) Schleiermacher stated the following: "Since the peace of Tilsit we have made tremendous progress, without revolution, without houses of parliament, even without freedom of the press. But always the people with the king, and the king with the people. Wouldn't one be out of one's mind to think that we would make more progress with a revolution? For my part I'm very sure always to be on the side of the king when I'm on the side of the intellectual leaders of the nation" (Friedrich Wilhelm Kantzenbach, *Schleiermacher* [Reineck bei Hamburg, 1967], p. 145).

39. CF, p. 557.

40. Barth, *Protestant Thought*, p. 322.

41. CF, p. 531.

42. CF, p. 555.

43. CF, p. 549.

44. CF, p. 61.

45. CF, p. 611.

46. Hugh Ross Mackintosh, *Types of Modern Theology* (London, 1937), p. 82.

47. Emmanuel Levinas quoted in José Miranda, *Marx and the Bible* (Maryknoll, 1974), p. 266. In developing a biblically grounded option to the Schleiermacher approach I find myself close to Miranda's deep involvement in the biblical struggle for justice.

48. CF, p. 346.

49. CF, p. 347.

50. CF, p. 348.

51. Macquarrie, *Thinking about God*, p. 165.

52. Ibid.

53. CF, p. 565.

54. CF, p. 138.

55. Yorick Spiegel, *Theologie der bürgerlichen Gesellschaft: Sozialphilosophie und Glaubenslehre bei Friedrich Schleiermacher* (Munich, 1968), pp. 21–31.

56. Ibid., p. 162f.

57. Ibid., p. 235ff.

58. Herbert Marcuse, *Reason and Revolution* (Boston, 1968), p. 14f. As in note 10, I need to stress that there has been too little research on the

historical background of Schleiermacher's stance on this point. There is even less theological research on the consequences in German culture. One non-theological volume I found very helpful in this regard is Fritz K. Ringer, *The Decline of the German Mandarins: The German Academic Community, 1890–1933* (Cambridge, 1969).

CHAPTER FOUR

# The Bible and
# the Marxist Revolution

The Bicentennial jolted us into remembering what we often
forget: that we are *heirs* of a revolution. We have a stewardship
here. The modern political and economic world came into being
through revolution. Theology was not left untouched. And yet we
often act as though theology had nothing to do with the particular
revolutionary dynamics that brought the modern world into being. We can partly understand why Schleiermacher seemed unable to catch on to what was happening. It was all still very fresh
and new. There was too much of the revolutionary newness to
appropriate. Schleiermacher got hung up on the scientific "revolution," the change of worldview, and the consequent changes in
attitude.

In our time we cannot avoid the wider picture. Actually there is
little difficulty in understanding why this is so. In a sense it is there
for anyone to behold who has eyes to see. Hannah Arendt made
the point very strongly: "Even if we should succeed in changing
the physiognomy of this century to the point where it would no
longer be a century of wars, it most certainly will remain a century
of revolutions. In the contest that divides the world today and in
which so much is at stake, those will probably win who understand
revolution."[1] What theology needs to make clear to itself today is
twofold: *(a)* Christians cannot understand revolution without the
Bible. *(b)* Christians can no longer understand the Bible without
the modern history of revolution—which includes the Marxist
revolution.

We cannot understand the revolution without the Bible. Our

difficulty as a people here is that the *colonization* of North America had much to do with the Bible, but the *revolution* of 1776 did not. Afterwards we interpreted the 1776 revolution through the grid of colonial Bible-reading. But that largely confused things. The Pilgrims had seen New England as the place of a covenant between God and the people, just like the covenant with Moses and the people of Israel. The first covenant had led to the conquest of Canaan, the promised land. The new covenant led to the conquest of the goodly land called America. That myth prevailed not only in New England. It took hold of the imagination of many immigrant groups. It plays a significant role, for example, in the moving tale by O. E. Rölvaag, *Giants in the Earth* (1927), which describes the settlement of the Dakota territory in the late nineteenth century by Norwegians and other European immigrants.

It is a fact that today many in this country still think of themselves as a covenant people in Moses' terms. But they forget that the political founding of the nation in 1776 had little to do with the Bible. The revolution was basically a "secular" event. Politically we have been moving along in a momentous extension of this very eighteenth-century secularization—without ever, on grounds of the Bible, radically thinking through what happened since.

To continue unthinkingly can mean only to extend Puritan civil religion into the late twentieth century. Whatever may happen in this regard in the country as a whole, the church had better try to bring the Bible and revolution into a new interaction. Without the Bible, the creative potential of our revolution seems to be escaping us more and more. This does not mean that we should claim the revolution for ourselves as being Christian or divine. As we said, it was a secular event. There should be no "mixing of categories." What we can learn from the American revolution is that human beings assumed responsibility for self-government. What Christians can derive from it is that they too had better take their particular historical assignment in the modern context seriously.

Part of the genius of the American revolution is the interdependence between freedom on these shores and the fate of other peoples. Wrote Thomas Jefferson: "Let us consecrate a sanctuary for those whom the misrule of Europe may compel to seek happiness in other climes. This refuge once known will produce reaction on the happiness of those who remain there, by warning their taskmasters that when the evils of Egyptian oppression become heavier than those of the abandonment of country, another Canaan is open where their subjects will be received as brothers, and secured against like oppressions by a participation in the right of self-government." Jefferson concludes with a very pungent point: "A single good government becomes thus a blessing to the whole earth, its welcome to the oppressed restraining within certain limits the measure of their oppressions."[2] We still have a notion of interdependence with other peoples. The question is always to what extent we are willing to make it real. The question is also to what extent we are willing to see the interdependence of the American revolution and the Marxist revolution. The Bible compels us to think hard about the meaning of secular events.

As one reflects on the American revolution from the biblical perspective there seems no reason for doing more than acknowledging the secular integrity of the event: *revolution in America was the overthrow of overlords for the self-government of the people in a new world of plenty.* In order to understand the Marxist revolution we need to get two points of the American revolution into clearer focus.

1. There is a strong current in the American consciousness that admits that the revolution was never over. So Benjamin Rush wrote in 1786, ten years after the revolution had begun: "A belief has arisen that the American Revolution was *over.* This is so far from being the case that we have only finished the first act of the great drama." There is no absolute criterion by which we could determine whether we are now into the second or third act. With some justification one might call the Emancipation of the slaves in 1863 the second act, in keeping with revolutionary expectation expressed, for example, by one of the founding fathers, John Adams, as the emancipation of slavish humankind. Today we are face to face with the emancipation of the slavish part of humankind *all over the earth.* That may well be part of the third act, begun

in the Marxist revolution. As to its dynamics we have no choice. We are all heirs of the American overthrow of bondage. That dynamic, once having entered the mainstream of the global community, is inescapable.

2. Without the experience on these shores that something really new could happen there would have been no sense of revolution. There were no revolutions in the Middle Ages or the Reformation, only rebellions. With the discovery of the new world a new way of acting seemed possible. The cyclical patterns of persistent bondage could be broken. A new order of things could appear, a *novus ordo seclorum*.

Today there are no longer new worlds to conquer by large masses of people. Emigration to the moon or Mars, once dreamed about, is out of the question thus far. We tend to sit back in God's country and congratulate ourselves on our achievements, enjoying our affluence. The revolution of interdependence Jefferson spoke of, built into the revolution of independence, is easily put out of our minds. But the Marxist revolution keeps us from forgetting it completely.

## THE MARXIST REVOLUTION AS MIRROR

In many contexts in the United States one dare not even breathe the name of Karl Marx or talk about socialism. I am not going to claim that the Marxist revolution is a direct descendant of the American revolution. Yet there are a number of connections, so that one should not be too squeamish about the name.

Karl Marx for several years was European correspondent of a New York newspaper. Early in his life he had claimed that socialism and communism "did not orginate in Germany, but in England, France, and North America." In North America! It cannot be denied that American models were sponsors at the baptism of German socialism. There are some "roots" of the Marxist revolution in our own revolutionary history, even if we may not want to agree with C. Wright Mills, who claims that the works of Marx "clearly and consistently embody the secular humanism of the West."[3] The American revolution had raised the question of political freedom in the new world. The Marxist revolution raised the question of socioeconomic freedom as a political freedom in the old world. By now that question also impinges on the new world, and on many other parts of the world as well.

It is not for theology to claim that Karl Marx got his ideas from the Bible. We all are familiar with the old ministerial cliché that the Marxists cribbed our notes. The point is rather that those who read the Bible ought to have been able to see what Marx saw so well—that the poor and oppressed have a claim on justice. The Marxist revolution holds up a mirror to the church. The revolutionary thrust unleashed by the visionaries of the new world, which impinged on Karl Marx, is an eye-opener for Chrisitans. This does not mean that we should fuse the justice of the God of the Bible with modern revolution, which usually results in a Christian ideology for revolutions—no theological gain at all. Rather, Christianity needs to own up to its very own revolutionary dynamic. Where divine justice is not embodied by the church, people outside the church take matters into their own hands. This is the story of Karl Marx.

Karl Marx (1818–1883) enters the scene when the American revolution is not even half a century old. Born in Trier, he attends hometown schools and then studies in Bonn and Berlin. Due to a concatenation of events largely beyond his control he is unable to land the academic post for which he prepares himself. Of Jewish descent, he also has to face the horror of being a racial misfit in a society extremely race-conscious. Forced to leave Germany as a journalist (the job he takes up to make a living), he becomes an exile and little more than a pauper in Paris, Brussels, and finally London, where he dies. Thrust by fate on the marginal side of life, he needs no great extra push to discover the proletariat, the vast masses of people condemned to poverty by industrialization on the European mainland and the British Isles.

Marx admits what a lot of religious people in Europe in his day were unwilling to admit, and what a lot of religious people in this country are still unwilling to admit today: that industrial society creates poverty cycles, vicious circles of want in which poor people are virtually ensnared.

Jefferson knew very well that Europe was in trouble, that there was tremendous oppression. Fifty years later it was much worse. Industrialization had uprooted vast masses of people and made them destitute in ever-growing slums. Those poor who crossed the Atlantic had America. The poor that could or would not cross the Atlantic had Karl Marx. We need to recall the vast immigrations from Europe in the middle and late nineteenth century. The dynamic we have in Europe for revolution is part of the revolutionary dynamic that brought this body politic into existence. It is also part of the mindset that got into the Declaration of Independence: In order to secure rights of life, liberty, and the pursuit of happiness governments are instituted by men, deriving their just powers from the consent of the governed. Whenever any form of government becomes destructive of these ends it is the right of the people to alter or abolish it.

The dynamics of the European revolutions is similar to that of the United States: *revolution in Europe is the overthrow of overlords for the self-government of the people in the old world of scarcity.* The scarcity factor makes for the only initial difference in revolution between the two continents.

The revolutionary impetus in Europe was mediated through the French revolution. Just like the American revolution, it was a struggle for freedom. But it took place on a continent where there was no immediate abundance available. It paid no attention to the scarcity factor. Hannah Arendt comments:

> The young Marx became convinced that the reason why the French revolution had failed was that it had failed to solve the social question. From this he concluded that freedom and poverty were incompatible. His most explosive and indeed most original contribution to the cause of revolution was that he interpreted the compelling needs of mass poverty in political terms as an uprising, not for the sake of bread or wealth, but for the sake of freedom as well. What he learned from the French revolution was that poverty can be a political force of the first order. . . . Poverty itself is a political, not a natural phenomenon, the result of violence and violation rather than of scarcity.[4]

The American revolution would be successful largely because it could solve part of the social question, in part for Europe as well. Many of our American forebears came through Ellis Island in the context of this very dynamic. On these shores they did not have to face European scarcity as a political factor. Marx and his comrades on European shores still had poverty to battle.

This is the crucial point. We did not have to struggle with the same sociopolitical dynamic as Europe because of material blessings not of our own making. But poverty in Europe and other parts of the world did not go away. The Marxist revolution, as it were, began in Europe in 1848 and has continued since in countless ways. In 1917, in the October Revolution, Russia was the first country to institutionalize the Marxist revolution; this is a historical "accident" one needs to acknowledge the way one acknowledges similar accidents of history. Other countries followed. What we need to see is the mirror the revolutions are holding up to the church. In almost every instance the church had been on the side of the mighty, not with the poor. We cannot make Marx responsible for all the abuses of his theories. We would not want to make Jesus responsible for the Crusades or the Inquisition and all the dehumanization church history has brought. So there's just one point we want to let the Marxist revolution etch into our minds: in spite of all the drawbacks of Marxist theory we might discover, the fact that poverty is a political and not a natural phenomenon cannot be circumvented.

Poverty is a phenomenon that now also increasingly stares us in the face in North America. Humankind as a whole is facing it on a vast scale today. The Marxist revolution lets us not forget it as part of the modern human condition. As summed up by the American sociologist C. Wright Mills, Marx was saying:

> You do not have to be poor any longer. Everywhere men have always lived as exploiters and exploited. As long as the means of producing goods were not sufficient to provide for all, perhaps this evil condition was inevitable.
> It is no longer inevitable.
> You do not have to be poor.
> You are poor not because of anything you have done or

anything you have failed to do, not because of original sin or the Will of God or because of bad luck. You are poor because of economic and political conditions. These conditions are called capitalism. At first, capitalism was a great progressive force in man's history; under it men built enormous facilities for the production of all things they need. . . .

You do not have to be poor. The conditions that make you poor can be changed. They are going to be changed. . . . You are going to make a revolution. Those who rule over you and keep you poor will be overthrown. That is the next step forward in human progress. You are going to take that step.[5]

## THE BIBLICAL ANTIPOVERTY PROGRAM

The Marxist revolution could not be put in plainer terms. What about the Bible in the face of it?

The story of how the churches related to the poor in Europe has been told many times. It all went much along the line of Marx's complaint that the "English established Church will more readily pardon an attack on 38 of its 39 articles than on 1/39 of its income."[6] To illustrate Christian attitudes he had only to tell of everyday occurrences in plain view for all to behold: "In England even now occasionally in rural districts a laborer is condemned to imprisonment for desecrating the Sabbath by working his front garden. The same laborer is punished for breach of contract if he remains away from his metal, paper, or glass works on the Sunday, even if it be from a religious whim. The orthodox Parliament will hear nothing of Sabbath-breaking if it occurs in the process of expanding capital."

We have to keep this attitude of the churches in Europe in mind in order to understand why the Marxist revolution became inevitable. I am not about to rehash all of the sad history. Here we have only to remember the basic point, the failure of the church. There is a factor operative in our own revolutionary tradition that in part made the Marxist vision possible: the interdependence of peoples. This factor has a biblical precedent. The church's failure is partly due to forgetting this precedent.

Thomas Jefferson spoke of the interdependence of peoples. The Bible had already suggested in regard to the relationships between peoples: your fate is my fate; God in Christ united all people in one humanity. In regard to poverty this implies: your poverty is my poverty.

A few years ago I spoke to a ministers' group in North Carolina. The presentation was, in broad terms, on regeneration, certainly not on economics or politics. Only in passing I commented that our social structure is not perfect and that capitalism has drawbacks that even a regenerate person has to look at critically. Hardly was I through, when one of the brethren shot to his feet and exclaimed, "What have you got against capitalism? Why, God himself is a capitalist." Recently someone from West Virginia told me, "In our neck of the woods religion is God and the free enterprise system."

In many churches, the ideological use of the Bible as the book of God's covenant with the American people also involves God's covenant with the economic system of capitalism. Of course, the Bible is not a socialist book either. While there was no capitalism in its present form in those days, there was also no socialism. But in creative interaction with the cultures of its day the Bible witnessed to God's revolution. It very effectively pointed out that God does not consider poverty a natural phenomenon. Poverty was not something to be stoically endured. In this vein Mary's Magnificat rings out God's truth: "He has put down the mighty from their thrones, and exalted those of low degree; he has filled the hungry with good things, and the rich he has sent empty away" (Luke 1:52f.).

There is no promise in the Bible that the church can Christianize the social order. But it also does not promote fate: that things have to stay the way they are. Only with the modern revolutionary dynamic has the idea that things can be changed effectively entered into human consciousness. But the Bible knows that changing poverty involves political change.

There is obviously more than poverty that the Christian Gospel is concerned about; there is also sin, disobedience, pride, etc. But poverty is the touchstone of so much else; poverty breeds crime. It is the foil of greed and hardness of heart. So the Christian life centers around the struggle against poverty: "If any one has the world's goods and sees his brother in need, yet closes his heart against him, how does God's love abide in him?" (1 John 3:17). "Blessed are you poor, for yours is the kingdom of heaven" (Luke 6:20).

In many ghetto situations people are so physically down and out that they cannot even grasp the Gospel of salvation. Here the mission of the church is being completely revamped. The task involves not just the changing of a mental or psychological condition, but the changing of the human condition.

In answer to the question "Who is God?" we usually say: "God is love," in terms of 1 John 4:8. But the English word "love" does not convey the full meaning of *agape*. God is justice-love. In the Old Covenant God is thought of as habitation of justice (Jer. 50:7). This also extends into messianic reflection: "For unto us a child is born, to us a son is given; and the government will be upon his shoulder. . . . Of the increase of his government and of peace there will be no end, upon the throne of David, and over his kingdom to establish it, and to uphold it with justice . . . " (Isa. 9:6,7). Appealing to God's justice the prophets excoriate worship unrelated to justice: "Take away from me the noise of your songs. . . . But let justice roll down like waters . . ." (Amos 5:23f.). That strand is also heard in the oft-quoted words of Micah: "He has showed you, O man, what is good; and what does the Lord require of you, but to do justice . . . " (Mic. 6:8). That God is not sentimental charity but justice means that God gives each person her or his due and expects people to do the same.

It is in this framework that Jesus of Nazareth understood his mission. There is good reason to believe that he saw it primarily in terms of Isaiah 61:1–2: "To set at liberty those who are oppressed, to proclaim the acceptable year of the Lord." Jesus saw himself acting out the justice of God. It proved a tremendously difficult undertaking. The people as a whole were not ready for justice embodied in human life. Even the disciples misunderstood off and on. Without repentance there could be no understanding of God's justice (Mark 1:15). As the Jesus story gains momentum, it becomes clear that only a few understood, those who had been born anew (John 3).

The outcome of the story was a new reality of personhood focused in cross and resurrection and concretized in community. The neighbor is part of me. There *by* the grace of God go I (Matt. 25). Relationships between persons had been reversed. Not only were the last first, but the least were also part of human selfhood: "As you did it to one of the least of these my brethren, you did it to me" (Matt. 25:40).

Here the church's ministry becomes extremely difficult. There is no way of circumventing the praxis of God's identification with the poor in one's own life. A seminary degree, a B.D. or an M.Div., does not empower a person for the communication of God's battle with poverty. Ordination as such does not legitimate one's preaching. Neither does the constant study of exegesis or homiletics. It all hinges on participation in God's struggle. Obviously that cannot be produced in the pulpit as such. But a pastor who is not involved in God's battle against poverty has no authority in the pulpit or otherwise. A Christian not participating in God's battle has no power to bring others to Christ.

The mission of the church today is still seen too much in terms of home missions, making people feel happy, helping people to cope. All of this is subordinate to God's mission among suffering humankind righting the human condition. God is struggling on the frontier of human misery. God is drawing the church out of its self-seclusion into the woes and trials of the human family—out of ivory palaces into a world of woe. All comfort is subject to that dynamic of mission.

When the church had almost completely forgotten that mission, it was through the Marxist revolution that the church was reminded again of the biblical antipoverty program. God prepared a painful awakening.

## ANTIPOVERTY MISSION IN THE GLOBAL VILLAGE

There still exists a tremendous fear of Marxist revolution. I do not want to belittle its negative effects, a new totalitarianism, new bureaucracies, etc. We need to be fair, however. The 1917 revolution in Russia was not purely Marxist, but part of the self-reorientation of the Russian empire. Lately it has been similar with the Chinese. In the end, most of us can distinguish between what Marx wanted, and what politics has made of his ideas in old and new national empires.

It is important to keep in mind that the American revolution, by which U.S. citizens define their existence, and the Marxist revolution are not unrelated.[7] Both are part of the modern dynamic of the overthrow of overlords for the self-government of the people. As the American revolution teaches us the interdependence of oppressed peoples, the Marxist revolution injects political leverage into interdependence for overcoming poverty. Today an ever-shrinking globe makes the political dimension of poverty inescapably part of the fabric of every human life. Obviously Christians cannot solve all issues involved. But the church can bring the biblical antipoverty program into creative interaction with world need. The political responsibility of rich Christians for the world's poor can no longer be flouted.

The rich Christians in this country can no longer stand back from the struggles of the poor and say: It's none of our business. Obviously the church cannot do what governments will not do. It's not the business of the church to try to be the perfect United Nations. But by the same token Christians cannot turn around and say: We've got to fight the poor. That was what hurt us in Vietnam. The freedom struggles of the poor are part of the dynamic this country helped to unleash. The church is compelled to tell itself: The God of justice makes the fate of all people my fate. The church is not the burdenbearer of humanity. God bears the burdens. But God asks Christians to share in burdenbearing. God's justice embodied in Christ made St. Paul learn in his mission to the Global Village of his day that not one person dare be dehumanized. The church can do something about it. Through God's justice embodied in Christ the church says to all peoples: Your fate is our fate. This implies: Your poverty is my poverty, and I can change part of it. The change, as Marx rightly saw, involves changing political structures.

All this does not mean that Christianity is only a this-worldly ethic. The church does not proclaim that once people are fed,

God's kingdom has come. Christianity offers eternal life. But by this offer it means that *this* life has eternal value. This is what we are struggling about in the church today. We are digging in for the long haul. Its going to be a long, drawn-out struggle, but a joyous struggle.

We are not saying that we have to out-socialize the socialists or take over the Marxist revolution. We are also not saying that the church can transform the political dynamic.[8] What we can do is take seriously the unbelievably potent dynamic the modern world has thrust upon us. It has created the Global Village. Yet the creativity of the biblical truth is also there to be tapped by all peoples. What is the chief end of man? asks the Westminster Shorter Catechism. The chief end of being human is to share in God's justice, and to enjoy it forever.

Can there be a creative interaction between the biblical anti-poverty program and revolution? In God's good time revolution has made the Christian community aware again of its major task. Through the processes of history God is waking up the church. Self-adulation in the churches has made us feel at ease in Zion. The American revolution is not over, said Benjamin Rush. By the same token, the Marxist revolution is not over. There are 700 million illiterates in the Third World, 100 million more than twenty years ago. There are 230 million jobless in the Third World. Among the young people in Detroit, there are up to 40 percent jobless. Someone remarked recently: Any problem today not set forth in terms of the whole world is a problem badly posed.

In it all, the church is not even in a holding pattern. It is a losing proposition. "Assuming the present trend continues," claims Walbert Bühlmann, "experts predict that if Christians were 34 percent of the world population in 1900 and 31 percent in 1955, they could be only 16 percent in 2000."[9] The problem of missions in the future is largely a problem of tackling poverty. It is also a problem of facing the exploitation of women and of coming to terms with racism. The whole point is that the church cannot escape committing itself to the emancipation of the slavish part of humankind all over the earth. The Christian revolution could be just beginning.[10]

## NOTES

1. Hannah Arendt, *On Revolution* (New York, 1967), p. 8.
2. E. Boykin (ed.), *Wisdom of Thomas Jefferson* (New York, 1941), p. 6. It is clear to me how limited the views of a slave owner had to be. But the fundamental insights of the North American revolutionaries dare not be overlooked, however limited their own embodiment of these insights.
3. C. Wright Mills, *The Marxists* (New York, 1962), p. 24.
4. Hannah Arendt, *On Revolution*, pp. 56f.
5. Mills, *The Marxists*, p. 32.
6. Karl Marx, *Capital* (New York, 1906), p. 15.
7. Karl Marx himself was very much inclined to stress the interdependencies: "As in the 18th century, the American war of independence sounded the tocsin for the European middle-class, so in the 19th century, the American civil war sounded it for the European working-class" (Ibid., p. 14).
8. Cf. Paul Lehmann, *The Transfiguration of Politics* (New York, 1975). I do not know what "transfiguration of revolution" by the saving story of the Gospel really means (p. 239). But Paul Lehmann was one of the first to show the need for relating Christianity and modern revolution. That is a great merit.
9. Walbert Bühlmann, *The Coming of the Third Church* (Maryknoll, 1977), p. 143.
10. It is clear to me that there have also been other interpretations of the relationship between the American revolution and the European revolutions. See, for example, Abraham Kuyper, *Lectures on Calvinism* (Grand Rapids, 1931), pp. 85ff. The issue is to analyze the relationship time and again from new perspectives. There is a basic interdependency between the two continents that has not as yet been exhaustively explored.

# CHAPTER FIVE

## *Liberation and Imagination*

" 'Escape God's justice, flee to his love,' said a billboard on a churchlawn I had to pass almost every day on my fieldwork assignment this summer," one of our students remarked upon her return to classes this fall. "For the first time I really understood what the struggle of liberation theology is all about in our churches."

For the popular mind in this country there is little doubt that the Gospel of salvation is all about l-o-v-e. It oozes out of many pulpits. It congests our airwaves. It strangely warms our TV screens.

Here is where the heart of the United States churches beats spiritually. Yet for some time there has been a disturbing note in it all. The mind of the church has been jarred by liberation theology. There is some homegrown liberation theology, and then there is the import from Latin America and other parts of the Third World.

Right now there is much criticism of liberation theologies. They seem to represent too many claims or interests prohibiting a uniform assessment. But if one seriously examines the various contexts in which liberation theologies arise, objections diminish. The most convenient way to get rid of liberation theology thus far, as we noted in the introduction, has been to set up a strawman, and then to proceed to knock it down. In *Interpretation*, to point to another example, Stanley Hauerwas refers to a book by Paul Lehmann (who to my knowledge never claimed that he was propounding a liberation theology, but who in this context seems to appear under its auspices) and lifts from it a quote by Camilo Torres whose forte seems to have been a theology of revolution.[1]

The emerging composite is then used by Hauerwas to make liberation theology look bad.

One way to proceed more fairly might be to distinguish between liberation theologies in the Third World and in North America and to tackle one of these theologies *in regard to its particular context*. The purpose of this chapter is to show how some North American liberation theology has to differ from Latin American liberation theology to a certain extent. As a test case we suggest a consideration of the way the Bible is used.

The difference comes about partly because of the peculiar contextualization of systematic theology in this country today. We are struggling to find a new creative imagination to undergird Christian discipleship. Which root metaphor is most adequate for our understanding of God? Paul Ricoeur offers a helpful orientation point: "Any ethic that addresses the will in order to demand a decision must be subject to a poetry that opens up new dimensions for the imagination."[2] The opening up of new dimensions for the imagination is the foremost challenge of systematic theology as liberation theology in North America.

In a preliminary way we can state that liberation theology attempts to take into account the non-person as foundational in shaping the theological imagination.

## COUNTERPOINTS TO LIBERATION THEOLOGY

To be fair to Hauerwas we need to listen to what he has in his heart as he runs down liberation theology. The core of his case is a stimulating analysis of poverty and power in the New Testament, especially the Gospel of Luke. The basic shape of the imagination, however, that undergirds his case is different from that of liberation theology. So we get a principal assertion such as, "What charity requires is not the removing of all injustice in the world, but rather to meet the need of the neighbor where we find him."[3] In this kind of imagination-milieu it seems very reasonable that "the Christian is obligated to love the neighbor, not all men."[4] And in general no one could disagree, I suppose, that the Gospel "gives us the skill patiently to love and care for some when not all can be loved and cared for."[5]

Put simply on the level of an ethic that addresses the will, it appears obvious that charity does not require the removing of all injustice in the world. It is equally obvious that we are not asked to love all persons at the same time. But God's own battle against all injustice is certainly not completely dissociated from what Hauerwas calls charity. A subtle shift takes place here that is foreign to New Testament thought: away from God's battle for justice to our love of neighbor wherever we find the neighbor.

How helpful is it to use Christian language in such a way as to retain a semblance of truth while its real meaning is made to disappear? The Hauerwas case hinges on a charity that does not exist in the Bible in the shape he describes, as best I can tell. Much of his charity argument remains on the level of what we humans can or cannot do. So the claim is made that "charity for Christians is not something we wish to do, it is an obligation. We are commanded to be charitable. . . . Charity is required neither to justify our existence nor rid us of our guilt, but because it is the measure of being most like God. For we are commanded not to be revolutionaries, or to be world changers, but simply to be perfect."[6] Someone might ask: What could be wrong with all this; do not religionists use this type of language all the time? This is part of the problem. We use it so much we fail to notice the ideological smokescreen.

Indeed, God does not *command* us to be revolutionaries or world changers. But that seems so obvious it could hardly be the primary issue for the North American theological imagination. Might not the primary challenge rather be to focus on what God is doing? God changes the world in justice. It began for Christians in Messiah Jesus. In him the change was not primarily a matter of command, but of new creation—new human experience-structures in which we are invited to share. If anyone is in Messiah Jesus, this person is a new creation (cf. 2 Cor. 5:17). The struggle is over this shape of God's history. Hauerwas is also interested in God's history. But the great differences in theology, and the use of the Bible in particular, came about because God's history in Israel and in Messiah Jesus is understood in divergent ways.

## THE BIBLE IN LATIN AMERICAN
## LIBERATION THEOLOGY

God in Israel and in Messiah Jesus takes sides in the struggle for justice with non-persons (cf. Ps. 12:5; 34:6; Luke 6:20). This is the fundamental point for the new theological imagination. It is near tragic that the real causes for the rise of liberation theologies in the Third World are often almost tuned out, while flaws in their theological argument are immediately excoriated. We white Christians of the West often assume that what counts is correct theological ideas, regardless of how disorderly our lives may be. But the disorder of our lives has gotten out of hand, often victimizing those who find themselves on the receiving end of our superior political and economic power.

Steve Biko in South Africa, at the time of the writing of this chapter, is the latest of those Third World witnesses to lay down their lives for liberation.[7] Shortly before, Elisabeth Käsemann, daughter of Ernst Käsemann and social worker in Argentina, had her life snuffed out in a similar situation. We pay some attention to social disorders when we hear names we are somewhat familiar with. But it is only with faithful attention to the actual detail of social disorders in particular contexts that liberation theologies can be assessed with fairness. This pertains also to the use of the Bible in Latin American liberation theologies, where Third World exegetical concerns have been most fully advanced.

An example of fair evaluation is an article by J. Andrew Kirk, which begins with the revolution in theological methodology Latin American theologians want to achieve.[8] Solidarity with the oppressed involves a different starting point for work with the Bible. Here a kind of Kierkegaardian either/or arises. Either the theologian decides (1) to change the present sociopolitical order through the liberation of the oppressed or (2) to maintain the present order essentially as it is. The choice of the first option requires laying bare ideological perspectives that use the Bible to legitimate political and economic power.

In terms of the first option Hugo Assmann rejects the classical hermeneutical procedure that begins with the Bible and moves from there to the contemporary situation. Historico-critical perspectives today mediate the biblical message to the present situation in such a way that it provides the actual starting point. Assmann rather wants a particular contemporary praxis to perform the mediation. Revolutionary theory is for him the right hermeneutical key that concerns itself first with actual history and only secondarily with the past history of the Gospel. Verification of this hermeneutic is not found in the sources themselves, but in the concrete historical mediation of the present.

Gustavo Gutiérrez stresses the political dimension of the Gospel as part of its very essence, that is, not derived from any secular political option. José Miranda, on the one hand, attempts to discover a specific justice mode in biblical thought through objective historico-critical research while, on the other hand, stressing the doing of justice in the present situation as an inescapable obligation. He offers a hermeneutical circle in which apparently one can begin either from the biblical text or present reality. Finally Juan Segundo is shown to underscore the point that revolutionary commitment to liberation-exegesis means starting with Marxist analysis of present society as pre-understanding of the biblical text. Kirk observes that this looks very much like a parallel to Bultmann's view of pre-understanding in the demythologizing scheme.

The churches in Latin America have for years—in fact, for centuries—basically bypassed theological analysis of the poverty of the masses. In some Latin American countries not even minimal human rights are honored. The hermeneutic now developing is a hermeneutic *in extremis*, an attempt to understand the Bible among people pressed against the wall, people in prison, people shot to death. Difficulties for us begin at the point where there is either explicit or at least implicit expectation that in North America we could make this hermeneutic our own.

Situation analysis in North American theology is nothing new. It has usually proceeded under the aegis of liberal theology on grounds of scientific control of the subject matter, a control that is part of the social system.[9] The liberation struggle in the North

American churches is also directed toward this interdependency
of control in the entire system. So it is impossible for us to make
headway with the principle of the Latin American hermeneutic,
expressed, for example, in some reflections by Hugo Assmann:

> It is . . . false to state that the whole biblical framework, with
> its infinite variety of paradigms and situations, is an
> adequate basis for establishing a satisfactory complex dialec-
> tics of hermeneutical principles. The theology of liberation
> sees itself as critical reflection on present historical practice
> in all its intensity and complexity. Its "text" is our situation,
> and our situation is our primary and basic reference point.
> The others—the Bible, tradition, the magisterium or teach-
> ing authority of the Church, history of dogma, and so on—
> even though they need to be worked out in contemporary
> practice, do not constitute a primary source of "truth-in-
> itself."[10]

The complexity of the North American situation makes it possible
for this kind of perspective easily to be absorbed by the system.
Shifting from a Bultmannian pre-understanding of the Gospel to
a Marxist pre-understanding in the United States leaves the control principle of liberal theology intact and God just as dead. The
principle of scientific control in theological liberalism lets God do
only what it wishes. Unless in our situation the Bible functions as
primary "text" of God's action, all we end up with is our own
action.

## THE PECULIARITY OF
## THE NORTH AMERICAN CONTEXT

One thing we are learning in the struggles of the North American churches over liberation is that theology cannot be absorbed
into hermeneutic. The function of social analysis as well as
philosophical analysis or psychological analysis is ancillary. We
have just gone through a period of faithful and valiant efforts to
liberate theology from efforts beholden to culture as determina-

tive of the theological task. The social analysis of Karl Marx should not be excluded; in fact, it is crucial. But it has to come at its proper place. It dare not be the tail that wags the dog.

We occasionally hear it said that in the United States nothing can last more than ten years. As there is a built-in obsolescence of cars, so there seems to be also a built-in obsolescence of our more recent theologies. But basic theological commitments cannot function in terms of technological obsolescence. We need to recover the virtue of the perseverance of saints.

We need to learn to persevere in the battle H. Shelton Smith was already waging in the forties in trying to move beyond what he then called religious liberalism.[11] Its *credo* had also grown very much out of a particular kind of mediation of the present. While the same labels were not used, there was similar insistence on the right hermeneutical key in terms of the present. And *e*volutionary theory was appealed to rather than *re*volutionary theory. The doctrine of evolution had made a significant impression on the churches. In fact, theologians at the time also wanted to declare a kind of solidarity with people struggling for meaning. Evolutionary theory in theology concerned itself with actual history—only secondarily with the past history of the Gospel. G. Stanley Hall contended that as humankind "becomes truly civilized revolutions cease to be sudden and violent, and become gradually transitory and without abrupt change." On the premises of liberal anthropology insisting on the goodness of the human being with an inherent capacity for justice and benevolence, Henry Ware could claim "that if we take a fair and full view, we shall find that wickedness, far from being the prevailing part of the human character, makes but an inconsiderable part of it. That in by far the largest part of human beings, the just, and kind, and benevolent dispositions prevail beyond measure over the opposite."

In this milieu it becomes quite understandable that George A. Coe viewed the end of God's activity, the kingdom of God, simply in democratic terms. For him there was a direct equation between the biblical phrase "Kingdom of God" and what he called "democracy of God." Under this umbrella Christian nurture became "growth of the young toward and into mature and efficient devo-

tion to the democracy of God, and happy self-realization therein."
God finally was known largely in terms of social relations.

In this country, particularly in the South, the struggle of H.
Shelton Smith, among others, against an anthropocentric theology had its good reasons. Justice had not been realized in society.
The kingdom of God had not come, instead we had World War I
and World War II. The democracy of God did not evolve. The
verification of the liberal hermeneutic in the concrete historical
mediation of the present moment had proved utterly deceptive.
Thus H. Shelton Smith insisted: "Those who would have us
believe that new insights into the divine nature can be achieved
only after they have been realized within human relations, not
only deny the most characteristic aspect of prophetic religion;
they invert the order of moral insight."

In the North American context, one can forget the struggle to
overcome verification of Christian truth through concrete historical mediation of the present moment only at the peril of bolstering the legitimation of capitalist culture. It resulted in making the
divine the human writ large. Theologians who tried to control
insight into God's history in terms of contemporary mediations
ended up being all the more controlled by modern culture. *Vestigia terrent!*

## GOD'S HISTORY AND HUMAN HISTORY

Hauerwas asserts that liberation theology says something like
charity must be effective in the world. Against this position he pits
charity as ineffective in the world. But this point/counterpoint
argument leaves out the result of the North American struggle
against religious liberalism. It is not a matter of whether human
charity is effective or ineffective in the world, but whether God's
justice is in effect.

Theologians have heaped too much verbiage on top of the
elementary justice point. In the North American situation the
Exodus model is not helpful for understanding God's justice
battle. Some observers of the present scene suggest the Babylonian captivity as a more appropriate model. But all this modelling

keeps us in a strange Babylonian captivity of the theological mind. The Christian point begins with the liberating event that God acts independently of us in Messiah Jesus to bring about justice.

God's kingdom comes. God "has put down the mighty from their thrones, and exalted those of low degree" (Luke 1;52). We read through the Magnificat and find nothing that would make us look for God in human relations. As the Jesus story unfolds God continues to act independently of human beings. It grips the people. The poor and the oppressed grasp what is going on. The high and the mighty and the rich go empty away.

A strange struggle goes on. God reaches out to all to give each what is due. Obviously Jesus as a finite human being reaches only a few. But the story seems to imply that God is struggling to bring about justice for all. In cross and resurrection God continues the battle. Pentecost brings people from all quarters as equals into the new humanity. Next, the primitive church embodies God's justice by having all things in common. Soon it reaches out to the Gentile as well, making Gentile equal to Jew. In the process, the apostles lock horns with authorities, rulers, and powers that be. All this is "seeing through a glass darkly" what God is doing all along in history.

It is of secondary importance that human beings can share in this history only imperfectly. Human usurpation of God's prerogatives in this history is taken with great seriousness. Human failure is dealt with at the great price of God's own sacrifice of the Son on the Cross. And frail human life is not seen as final. The gift of God is not only forgiveness of sin, but eternal life in Messiah Jesus as joyful participation in God's battle for a prevailing humanity. There is only one point to human life on this earth: Participation in God's struggle for a life of justice.

As we said, whether the struggle for a just life is effective or ineffective is not the issue. The meaning of life is in the struggle. A false imagination distracts from it. "Escape God's justice, flee to his love" is premised on a false imagination. God's justice is not an antipode of God's love. It is here that the analysis of Marx has its definite place in North America. Here we also find common ground with Latin American liberation theology. José Míguez Bonino calls attention to "the different processes through which the oppressed were led to accept oppression by adopting the point of view of the dominant class, to internalize the oppressor's imposition of inferiority, to develop a slave consciousness. When this happens, every religious performance and observance (however profound and liberating may have been its original intention) becomes in that context the carrier of oppression, an instrument of spiritual enslavement. Domination becomes a religiously founded fact; the bond of oppression is divinely sealed."[12] The fusion of religion and domination as a factor that denigrates people—the oppressor in a way as much as the oppressed—is not as yet addressed in a North American hermeneutic. Hauerwas, suggesting that God "provides a savior that teaches us how to be weak without regret,"[13] seems unaware of the fact that we are still being caught in an imagination insensitive to the slave mentality. As there are injustices one cannot forget, there are weaknesses one can only regret. There are weaknesses that in full view of justice are horrendous sins.

When St. Paul finds his strength in weakness (cf. 2 Cor. 12:10), he does not mean he is "weak without regret." The apostles would never have been jailed had they been content with charity not upsetting political and ecclesiastical structures.

Religion in the churches creates an ideal world in which love and equality seem realized, while in the realism of everyday existence there is inequality and injustice running amok. Initially religion probably invested the misery of the human condition with a halo and served as opiate of the people. Today it is often opiate *for* the people, used by the powers-that-be to cover up the real human condition. Sin, usurpation of divine power in trying to play God with our neighbor, expresses itself brutally in the material conditions of production. Christians in modern industrial society participate in creating human misery and oppression. In the face of these harsh conditions charity only sublimates the misery.

Unmasking the ideological perspectives that use the Bible to legitimate political and economic power is primarily not related to changing the present order through the liberation of the oppressed as a *human* task, but to God's justice battle. In the North American situation we cannot take over José Miranda's claim that a person must regard human history "as his only church."[14] We cannot make Gustavo Gutiérrez's "self-liberation"[15] or Juan Segundo's notion of this world becoming the new heaven of God[16] our own. We need to focus on God's struggle in history creating a church in history that stands against our sinful history. Taking seriously the methodological mistakes of the past in North American theology we turn first to God's liberation, looking forward to the new heaven and the new earth.

## LIBERATION HERMENEUTIC

All this does not make us less combative in locking horns with the destructive forces of our sociopolitical and socioeconomic system. It is only to say that the battle inside the leading capitalist nation of the world is fiercer and more complex than meets the eye. American churches hardly suspect that in merely participating in the economic system they might be living in apostasy. The liberation theologian appears as a killjoy whose chief fear is that people get some fun out of religion. The issue is whether the church has not already been rejected by God. The church has often claimed that Israel *was* rejected. Why should not God be able to turn the tables on the church? "Judgment must begin at the house of God" (1 Pet. 4:17). All liberation theology tries to do is to give a researched account of it. In the process the method of systematic theology is changing. The *bouleversement* may also affect biblical studies, church history, and practical theology.

1. *The Praxis Task.* Paul Tillich reflected the conventional wisdom of the modern theological method when he promoted "a systematic theology which tries to speak understandably to the large group of educated people."[17] Obviously theology would want to speak *to* the educated. To whom else would it want to speak? But there is also a blindspot to be considered. *From where* does Tillich speak? The struggle of the non-educated does not appear in Tillich's range of vision. Yet for understanding the Gospel it is not primarily important *to* whom it might be addressed, but *from* whom it comes. It was shaped in praxis before it was written down. Thus it ultimately reflects the shape of Jesus' praxis in the struggle for justice. Non-persons were part of it on

the ground level. Since the struggle has never ceased as God's struggle, the Gospel is never merely past. For the church, God's activity is always the essence of history in the present moment. Unless the theologian shares in God's praxis today, it is impossible to develop a Christian theology. The non-person today is also included in the divine activity.[18] God does not prove to be Godhead primarily in overcoming anxiety,[19] but in battling injustice. The theologian not involved in God's battle against injustice among the oppressed understands the Bible in a completely different way. The God of the Bible is a universal justice God and thus a gracious God. Since theology seeks to reflect God's truth in universals, it today needs to understand the difference between elite-universals (notions pertaining only to the religious in-group) and people's universals (notions including the non-person).

2. *The Dogmatic Task.* The primary reason for systematic theology is not the need for a coherent worldview, but the battle between truth and untruth in God's struggle for justice. Theologians seeking a coherent worldview as primary objective of theological reflection usually make philosophy the model of theological truth. Christian theology generates its own model, however. Today it involves the dogmatic point that God's praxis in Messiah Jesus, Christopraxis, comes first. The basic theological truth cannot be absorbed in a hermeneutic, not even a liberation hermeneutic. The Christian traditions have attempted to bear witness to the basic truth. But they have to be critically examined time and again. Popes can err, councils can err, reformers can err. Obviously liberation theologians can err. But we have to take the risk of praxis seeking new understanding.

The new imagination looks for Messiah Jesus not just in past history in need of being helped along today by revolutionary theory (Assmann) nor outside of real history, teaching us to be weak without regret (Hauerwas). It is an attempt to get on new ground. It is not a *via media*, a way in between, on the same ground. What is at stake is a new Christology that, while not undoing the Chalcedonian tension and balance between the divine and the human, acknowledges the continuity of divine activity in Messiah Jesus in history. It depends on a strong doctrine of the Holy Spirit. What it teaches us is not how to be weak without regret (human perfection), but how God is just without regret. There is nothing we need to learn except how we can share in God's struggle for justice. Obviously all of this does not happen without love. But God's love is first of all justice-love, the love of justice. It pertains primarily not to retributive justice, but to distributive justice in the contemporary situation. This does not mean that there is a special Christian form of the social order. What we are freed for is making choices in keeping with God's battle for justice.

3. *The Social Analysis Task.* There can be no question that atonement, forgiveness of sins, and eternal life belong to God's distributive justice. That is one side of the coin. The other side is that God's love cannot be used to sublimate the misery of oppression. We need to be utterly alert to the social dynamics of conflict that sublimate love. Obviously the Gospel does not offer us a social program for the twentieth century. But Messiah Jesus does liberate us for justice.

Society at crucial points stands in flagrant contradiction to God's fundamental justice work. We are constantly tempted to take over the societal view of God and the human being and to legitimate it. Once we grasp what is going on, it does not take much to see the contradiction pervading the very recesses of our thought. We have to be able to make the point clear to church people at the grassroots level. A recent cartoon with two executives at a manager's desk sums it up, as one tells the other: "Before God made profits, he made production, and before production he made capital. So be it."[20] This is blasphemy. God is used to legitimate injustice. It happens all the time. As long as we do not labor over a new image of God and of the human being any deed of love will only sublimate the blasphemy.

The social analysis of Karl Marx is the pioneer tool in the West for unmasking the ideology that undergirds the unjust sociopolitical and socioeconomic structures. Here is where the harshest clash comes. God is not on the side of the system. God frees us to be rational about more just choices. We cannot turn around and take God to justify another social system. All we can try to do is to work for a social order in keeping with God's justice. While it is true that the libertarian societies of the West have produced the injustices that haunt us today, it does not follow that the liberties they have produced have to be used for creating more injustice. Various forms of socialism inspired by these liberties have been tried in the West. Governments have been formed by socialist parties with the support of Christians. They have not attained perfection. But they have tried to make justice the momentum of the social order—which is only to say that in our libertarian societies we already have options of social order which have been tried and have not been found wanting altogether.

It is also only too clear that the socialist societies of the East, in varying degrees, have created new injustices, in some with death by the millions. In this regard elementary decisions are in order. In the context of his visit to Hungary Billy Graham told *Newsweek*, "Every country I go into has some form of socialism—including the U.S. I've decided that if I am to have a world ministry, I'll have to leave political questions alone."[21] But in view of God's battle for justice, if the church wants to have a world ministry it cannot leave political questions alone. The theological point is not that Christians are commanded to be socialists. The theological point is that God liberates us for being rational about the justice battle.

In the political realm we need to make intelligent secular decisions, not religious decisions. It is a highly rational judgment that in the present situation of our country we cannot flinch from socialism. We need to draw out more fully the form of socialism already present among us. It means to tap the most creative liberties our country offers. Theology cannot escape this kind of social analysis. It would be fatal, however, if one were to pontificate in this regard. Speaking for myself, in terms of the above analysis I am a Christian for socialism. I see the drawbacks and know the price to be paid. But it is impossible to remain silent about religious blasphemy in U.S. capitalism. Our choices remain risky and imperfect. The question is which greater good can be obtained or which greater evil avoided. The situation is grave.

Liberation theology might be offering a new option for systematic theology. Beginning in praxis we arrive at a new Christology. That demands as a next step careful social analysis. It needs to be noted that in the process a new model of theology has probably also emerged. In conclusion, we can only briefly highlight what turns out to be the most complex dimension of the liberation theology effort in North America.

*a. Correlation Model.* When consistently applied the method of liberal theology has made correlation the principle of most of its systematic theologies. Schleiermacher correlated feeling and absolute causality. Macquarrie today views existence and Being in correlation.[22] Naturally all of us correlate faith experiences with the world around us. But correlation as a theological principle implies that beyond the language we use to express Christianity there lies a depth dimension to which it owes its existence. That depth-dimension is the real thing we must talk about. So in a theologian like Macquarrie, all the biblical words about God, Christ, Holy Spirit, or Creation and Redemption, are qualified as symbols. The biblical language in essence is *symbol language.* In each effort to think through a symbol, the theologian, as it were, re-turns to the reality dimension that counts, Being, the depth of Being, or holy Being, and transfers thought to it. There is always some turning back involved to a more primordial realm, a deeper dimension, a fuller being—some transference away from history. It is next to impossible on this model of theology to view God's struggle for justice as the heartbeat of history.

*b. Creed Model.* It is quite understandable that Karl Barth inveighed against the principle of this approach. It was ultimately putting the human being in control of the theological enterprise with few questions asked about the narrow Cartesian premises. Barth's diligence, his commitment to a cause, and the infinite filigree of argument in rejection of liberal theology have produced one of the classics of dogmatics in the history of the church. The model most pervasive in the final form of this opus is the Creed.[23] Much of neo-orthodoxy took its cue from this orientation. It does not take away from the greatness of Barth's achievement if one explains that this often led him to preference of the concept as the crucial language vessel of Christian truth. In the realm of concept everything ultimately has its place and is realized. Barth also made good use of metaphor in the many-faceted approaches of his work. But what dominates is *concept language.* When everything has been said and done a note of final consummation of God's work in the present rings through the use of biblical language that again makes it difficult to get hold of an ongoing struggle of God in history. "The strife is o'er, the battle done. . . ."

  *c. Gospel Model.* Correlation of faith and world or appropriation of credal concepts are not appropriate models for us today in this country. A few liberation theologies are trying to find out how the Gospel story itself functions as a model of theology. It appears that the primary intent of Gospel story language is not to make us look backward into some deeper realm of Being or to conceptualize Christian events. The Gospel language is predominantly *metaphor language.* The Gospel story in its manifold metaphorical forms wants to create new justice and embody it in this world.[24] New structures of human life experience are introduced that evoke a new history. A new reality is being created, not behind this world, but in this world.[25] It is this reality that turns the world into the public arena for God's justice.[26]

  The whole struggle over the place of story in theology seems to find new purpose right here.[27] The new imagination sees the Gospel metaphors embracing the non-person as constitutive of being human. The Chalcedonian Christology of true God and true man in one person is re-focused in Messiah Jesus, constituting true God and true history in one praxis of justice. The biblical language is now free to do what it is supposed to do—to shape theology in praxis. But we are still very much in the "birth pangs" stage.[28] All we can hope for in our time is that we no longer have to say: "Must then a Christ perish in torment in every age to save those that have no imagination?"[29]

## NOTES

  1. Stanley Hauerwas, "The Politics of Charity," *Interpretation*, 31:3 (July 1977), p. 252.
  2. Paul Ricoeur and Eberhard Jüngel, *Metapher: Zur Hermeneutik religiöser Sprache* (Munich, 1974), p. 70. The crucial theological point here at stake was brought out years ago by Karl R. Popper: "It is, I believe, perhaps the greatest strength of Christianity that it appeals fundamentally not to abstract speculation but to the imagination, by describing in a very concrete manner the suffering of man" (*The Open Society and Its Enemies* [New York, 1962], p. 357).
  3. Hauerwas, "The Politics of Charity," p. 258.

4. Ibid., p. 252.

5. Ibid.

6. Ibid., p. 258.

7. It is important first of all to *listen* to what the poor have to say. Otherwise we might simply continue to impose our vision of the social struggle on the actual struggle of the poor. Steve Biko made that point very clear for the South African situation: "This is white man's integration . . . in which black will compete with black, using each other as rungs up a step ladder leading them to white values. It is an integration in which . . . the poor will grow poorer and the rich richer in a country where the poor have always been black" (Basil Moore [ed.], *The Challenge of Black Theology in South Africa* [Atlanta, 1974], p. 40).

8. J. Andrew Kirk, "The Bible in Latin American Liberation Theology," in Norman K. Gottwald and Antoinette C. Wire (eds.), *The Bible and Liberation: Political and Social Hermeneutics* (Berkeley, 1976), pp. 157–65. I will follow the wording of the Kirk article rather closely if for no other reason than to call attention to a fair presentation of liberation theology emphases. The Kirk piece also brings a careful critique of Latin American positions.

9. I have tried to work this out more fully in "Liberation Hermeneutic as Ideology Critique?" *Interpretation*, 28:4 (October 1974), pp. 387–403.

10. Hugo Assmann, *Theology for a Nomad Church* (Maryknoll, 1976), p. 104.

11. H. Shelton Smith, *Faith and Nurture* (New York, 1941). For the overview see pp. 1–66. My own work in the South is in direct continuity with H. Shelton Smith's struggle.

12. José Míguez Bonino, *Christians and Marxists* (Grand Rapids, 1976), pp. 62f. There are always those who object to the use of the domination theme. It seems a sheer Marxist invention. But it has also played a significant role, for example, in hermeneutical reflection on modern science. See Hans-Georg Gadamer, *Truth and Method* (New York, 1975), who indicates that "the knowledge of all the natural sciences is knowledge for domination" (p. 409; cf. pp. 315, 323, 437, and 495).

13. Hauerwas, "The Politics of Charity," p. 257.

14. José Miranda, *Marx and the Bible* (Maryknoll, 1974), p. 227.

15. Gustavo Gutiérrez, *A Theology of Liberation* (Maryknoll, 1973), pp. 146 and 217.

16. Juan Luis Segundo, *Our Idea of God* (Maryknoll, 1974), p. 44.

17. Paul Tillich, *Systematic Theology*, III (Chicago, 1963), p. 4. Cf. Thorstein Veblen, *The Theory of the Leisure Class* (New York, 1953), pp. 235ff.

18. It is difficult to show in theology that this is still a point to be learned

unless the context for the point in our own ideologies is acknowledged. Paul Holmer, "About Black Theology," *Lutheran Quarterly*, 28:3 (August 1976), claims: "Black theology, if it wishes to make something manifest, needs to join in the many-sided and wide-ranging and subtly-hued interchange between present and past. This is what academic life is always about" (p. 236). Professor Holmer apparently has had what he claims were unfortunate experiences with students at Yale, experiences I have never run into in the South. In the end, his elaboration on these experiences leads to the invitation: Accept our academic life. However much one might sympathize with unfortunate experiences and however "wrong" the poor might be academically, is there no wrong in our imagination? Does not Mt. 7:3 about the speck in the brother's eye and the log in one's own eye apply also to academicians? Professor Holmer fears that "we doom ourselves to converting everything only to ideologies" (ibid.), a very understandable fear. But does not "what academic life is always about" also involve ideologies that need to be acknowledged exactly at this point? Would not our imagination have to change if we were to include the poor in our academic universals?

19. See John Macquarrie, *Principles of Christian Theology*, 2nd. ed. (New York, 1977), p. 86.

20. *Time* (August 16, 1976), p. 54. Obviously one should not try to "popularize" a scholarly treatise. The point is that theology in regard to social analysis needs to keep in tension grassroots perceptions and scholarly analysis. For the latter see, for example, Jürgen Habermas, *Knowledge and Human Interests* (Boston, 1971), and Paul Ricoeur, "Ethics and Culture," *Philosophy Today*, 17 (1973), pp. 153–65.

21. *Newsweek* (August 29, 1977), p. 70.

22. The basic model, of course, was developed in Friedrich Schleiermacher, *The Christian Faith* (Edinburgh, 1928).

23. An immediate access to this model is Karl Barth, *Dogmatics in Outline* (New York, 1949).

24. In many quarters today there is an attempt to understand the use of metaphor in religion in a new way. See Wesley A. Kort, *Narrative Elements and Religious Meaning* (Philadelphia, 1975): "Although metaphor is a category familiar to literary critics and theorists, particularly to those oriented to lyric poetry, it is inadequately appreciated by theorists of religion, and it may be possible to suspect that what are taken in religious life and thought to be symbols may occasionally really be metaphors" (p. 7).

25. A move away from "symbol" in Christian theology may be noted in several contexts. See W. Willimon, "Tillich and Art: Pitfalls of a Theological Dialogue with Art," *Religion in Life*, 45:1 (Spring 1976), pp. 72–81.

26. Here again there is a tremendous tension between the popular mind and the theological wrestling for clarity. From the grassroots perspective Eric Sevareid recently made a telling comment in regard to the Third World: "I refuse to feel guilty about their poverty. . . . Look at black Africa. There's very little there that's worth much in 20th century terms" (*Time*, December 12, 1977, p. 111). It is impossible for theology to inject the guilt factor. It has to bracket it out. The question pertains rather to God's distributive justice. In strict systematic theology terms, we are not much beyond where Paul Tillich was when he tried to reconcile love and justice in God, yet under the aegis of *retributive* justice. See Paul Tillich, *Systematic Theology*, II (Chicago, 1957): "Justice is the structural form of love without which it would be sheer sentimentality" (p. 174). Much work needs to be done on this issue from the systematic theology angle.

27. Dietrich Ritschl and Hugh O. Jones, *"Story" als Rohmaterial der Theologie* (Munich, 1976). Part of the experiment of my *Liberation Theology* (New York, 1972) was to cast Christian theology in the model of the Gospel story.

28. See my article, "Birth Pangs: Liberation Theology in North America," *Christian Century*, 93:41 (December 15, 1976), pp. 1120–25.

29. George Bernard Shaw, "Saint Joan," in *The Oxford Anthology of English Literature*, vol. 2 (London, 1973), p. 1609.

Note: I am grateful to *Interpretation* for permission to reprint the material of this chapter from vol. 32:3 (July 1978).

# CHAPTER SIX

# Biblical Metaphors Creating
## the Justice Church: A United Church of Christ
## Statement as Test Case

Who benefits from the enterprise called theology that we have been engaged in for several chapters? Seminary students? Theologians talking to themselves? The basic purpose of theology is to reflect in concert with the church on matters of Christian thought and action.

To talk about *the* church, however, is dangerous, as we discovered in the first chapter. There are many churches, or denominations. So as we wrestle with the notion of the church, we are tempted to focus on what is *common* to many churches. But we have not as yet reached that commonality in concrete unity.

In a recent article, "Denominations: Surviving the '70s," Martin E. Marty observes that "denominationalism outlasts all the theologies designed to replace it."[1] This is an elementary insight that the theological enterprise needs to think long and hard about. Without the quiet art of seeing the denomination as the place where the issues of justice and power have to be fought out theologically, little progress will be made.

The process of learning involved in these chapters moves through several stages to the point where one denomination is used as a testing ground for understanding the new function of the church. The United Church of Christ statement (see Appendix), worked out in a small seminar, is not unique. Other churches are engaged in similar efforts. But the very newness of the denomination makes for easy access to observable data. The statement itself was occasioned by the need to recapture the teaching momentum of the United Church of Christ. Two decades of strong church activism had left a number of lacunae in the reflective process. As the layperson quoted in the first chapter put it, we were doing all kinds of good things, but often for the wrong reasons.

The United Church of Christ obviously cannot get back to primitive Christianity. The appearance of the Constantinian church in the fourth century changed the function of the church. The growth of the denomination on this continent gradually changed the absolutist and authoritarian status of the church, but it did not necessarily undo its Constantinian function as legitimator of societal values and structures. Much historical work still needs to be done in relating the Puritan beginnings to where the denominations are heading today. But some fundamental understandings of the new situation are at least tangible.

Catapulted into the global village, the church is changing. It is inevitable that the churches come closer again to the struggle of primitive Christianity. The new happening needs to be more fully articulated. The function of the church is only in the process of being realized; so too is the function of theology.

What the book up to this point generates is largely an *un*learning process. It relates to the fact that the backbone of the old approach we reviewed in Chapter One has not been broken in our basic theological hermeneutic in this country. Langdon Gilkey made a tremendous thrust in the direction of the actual church, as we pointed out. But in his most recent work, *Reaping the Whirlwind*, the orientation remains Tillichian insofar as ontological analysis of society antecedes any specific reflections on the church. The beginning point of the book is an attempt to "evidence" the ultimate as part of historical experience: "Ingredient in our experience of history and of politics is a dimension of ultimacy and of sacrality."[2]

While the tensions of the historical struggle are referred to, even in terms of class struggle, the self-contradictions of the church in history are not the primal orientation point. What is more, while there are ample references to the enslaved, oppressed, or exploited, they are not the cutting edge of the hermeneutical starting point. How can the church minister to the world without losing itself? That was a crucial question for Gilkey a decade ago. But one can keep on talking to the world without ever finding the church.

We dare not look at the church simplistically. We do however understand a few things today that were inaccessible, for example, to Paul Tillich. We see now how his ontological analyses contributed to an ideological veneer that covered up the reality of our society. We are realizing that without direct encounter with the exploited in our theological method at the beginning, we ultimately stay withdrawn in our own group or class, buttressed in a fortress of sheer self-interest.

We need to be very clear about our goals. Today, after the failure of the great aspirations of the sixties to reform society, we hear again much talk about changing individuals. But all of this has been tried and found wanting. Said Orestes Brownson: "There is no such thing as reforming the mass without reforming the individuals who compose it."[3] The crusades of the churches to reform the masses by reforming individuals cannot be our mandate. And seeking to Christianize the social order, the way Rauschenbusch wanted to,[4] has also not proved very helpful.

The issue for the theologian or any thinking Christian today is whether the church can be the just church. That may not seem like very much. But if for Gilkey in the sixties the identity of the church was at stake, it is even more at stake in the eighties. Right now we have to battle for the identity of the church in society almost "recklessly," regardless of whether it immediately helps society or not. Purity of heart is to will one thing, said Kierkegaard. The trouble with the churches is that they are trying to do too many things at the same time. While trying to be church, many a church is also casting a roving eye on all kinds of tasks in society a church is incapable of solving *as church.*

## LET THE CHURCH BE THE JUST CHURCH

What *can* a church do? There is no thing too small in a church, no thing too big, that it would not have to be thought through theologically, that is, in relation to how God's self-realization in history appears in it. To think theologically is not to play God. It is simply thinking clearly about God's presence in the life of a woman dying of cancer, or of a father whose son is a dope addict, or the struggle of a Chilean for human rights, or the mind of a person caught in a lie. What is it that ties all of this together and makes sense of it?

Something new has to happen corporately in a denomination to make headway. When two years ago, in May 1976, with some prodding by the denomination, several ministers and theologians of the United Church of Christ gathered, together with church staff, to tackle this very issue, it resulted in the 1978 seminar report, "Toward the Task of Sound Teaching in the United Church of Christ," a nine-page paper submitted to the UCC Office for Church Life and Leadership for use in the teaching contexts for which this office is responsible.

The first two decades in the life of our new denomination, 1957–77, had passed. It was a good time to take stock. There is an introductory section, followed by an attempt to set the framework of sound teaching in terms of the two decades. Next we outline the present network of our denomination where the potential for sound teaching is located. Then we cover what we called "Liberation Affirmation," which likewise furnishes the core of the last chapter of this book. In a brief conclusion we sketched those areas where further work needs to take place. (It will be helpful for the reader from this point on to turn to the statement and especially to continue to check the "Liberation Affirmation.")

The premise of our statement is that the church today requires us to do hard thinking about justice. The justice issues arise in regard to three major challenges for the church: *State, Culture,* and *Ministry*. This is no idle talk in the UCC. The harsh clashes of sound teaching are emerging exactly in church/society interdependencies; we can no longer dodge clear commitments to the oppressed. "Church and society are caught in increasing conflict." The Wilmington Ten's struggle in the United Church is one illustration. The Human Sexuality report approved by the 1977 General Synod as a study for the whole UCC fellowship is another. The church is trying to act in terms of justice. But is it clearly grasping what it is doing?

Here is where theology needs to be renewed, since "God calls upon us to give a new acount of our hope lest we be 'tossed to and fro and carried about with every wind of doctrine' (Eph. 4:14)." The new account centers in the struggle for justice. From the many dimensions we talked about during the time of our gatherings in Seminar I we singled out the most pressing ones. The thoughtflow in each section of the statement is from God to the church—the corporate reality that witnesses to God's self-realization in history and seeks to embody God's reality.

We immediately stress God as Justice. We did not intend to exclude other descriptions of God. But we wanted to underscore that justice is God's very character, not merely an attribute. The statement draws together several strands of biblical thought often overlooked. Isaiah 45:21 emphasizes: "There is no other god besides me, a just God and Savior." Jeremiah 50:7 speaks of God as "habitation of justice." The same theme appears in Psalm 10:18, stressing God's activity: "Lord, . . . thou wilt do justice to the fatherless and oppressed." The appeal to God as justice involves the point that God looks out for the rights of the poor; it is of the very essence of God that this is so; it is part of God's salvation of the people.[5]

In this respect there is a significant change of emphasis from the neo-orthodox approach. Reinhold Niebuhr, for example, in *Moral Man and Immoral Society*, claimed: "A rational ethic aims at justice, and a religious ethic makes love the ideal. A rational ethic seeks to bring the needs of others into equal consideration with those of the self. The religious ethic (the Christian ethic more particularly, though not solely) insists that the needs of the neighbor be met, without careful computation of relative needs."[6] Much of this approach still prevails in many quarters of the church. The premise is that God in Christ is completely removed from the immediate claims of justice. It is love that meets the needs of a human being "without carefully weighing and comparing [these] needs with those of [God's] self. It is therefore ethically purer than the justice which is prompted by reason."[7] Thus God works in the church in one way and in society in another.

There is no good reason, however, why there should be a fundamental difference between the basis of a rational ethic and the basis of a religious ethic. God is at work realizing Godhead in history, in society as much as in the church. So Christians too had better be rational (not just religious), clear in thinking, weighing choices and values for church involvement in society.

Preaching and teaching in the church needs to be done in regard to the *one* work of God in history where God stands up for the weak and supports their just cause. Justice provides for love as universal mandate.

In the statement we expound the implications of the acknowledgment of God as justice. We do not want to say that God is on the side of India or Bangladesh rather than the United States. All we want to uphold is that the meaning of life does not consist in making might right, "but in struggling with God for justice among all peoples." Might makes right? No. Right makes right. God establishes divine rights in the world. Justice for the church is human rights on the basis of divine rights. God battles for the basic right of each human being to abundant life. It is only that the human enterprise is often turned against God's intention. It is usually the state that turns out to be the human means of thwarting God's intention for just life. The church often falls in line. So we say, "As a sociopolitical and socioeconomic institution, the church is implicated in the evils of the state."

The church is not a safe refuge from the real world. Politics reaches into every business meeting, budget meeting, or annual conference meeting. There is no easy way to distinguish between what happens in the church and the state. So the church is called to witness to God as justice in the state as well as in its own midst. Everywhere it is "called to serve God." What the institution of the state finally stands for is not principally different from what the church stands for: the dignity of human life.

We mention in the statement two evils that are compounded by our "state," racism and sexism. Other "evils" could have been mentioned. Sufficient unto the day are two evils thereof. We did not want to wallow in the negative. Our point was to stress that God is taking sides in the increase of personhood.

Since some of the models of how we relate as people reflect the basic shortcomings of our state system as legitimation of the ideology of capitalism—namely, limitless profit-making as the meaning and be-all of life—we had to point to an alternative. *Sixty*

*Minutes* early in 1978 carried a story about the Daisy Chain in the oil business: almost limitless profiteering, passing on false price increases to the electricity consumer involving millions of dollars; similar price increases were made by Texaco and Exxon during the oil embargo a few years ago. While there is no perfection in any social system, we can work for a system open to God's justice in history—an endless task.

If God in the world is battling for justice, as we see by the eyes of faith, the church cannot but be a *covenant of justice*, that is, people who join in God's struggle for the new age of justice. Our motivation is Jesus of Nazareth as Messiah of this covenant.

*Messiah* Jesus is a metaphor. Messiah and Jesus of Nazareth do not naturally belong together. The Messiah was expected as a brilliant supernatural figure, not as a nobody from Podunk. The new age of righteousness and glory was to come to Israel in a vast sweep of mythical events. Now a nobody from Nazareth takes up the task and embodies the messiahship in constant struggle for divine rights as the basis for human rights. It is with the authority of the one who is engaged in the justice battle that Messiah Jesus demands: "Seek first the kingdom of God and God's justice, and all other things shall be added to you" (Matt. 6:33).

The metaphor, Messiah Jesus, is "intent upon" creating the Justice Church among us. The human figure of Jesus is no longer present. But the imagination is spurred on to justice as it discovers that in a human being God was incarnate to make justice real.

The metaphor that creates the just community is crucial. Everything hinges on it. During the time of neo-orthodoxy there was no great expectation for a more specific qualification of the church. In the early days of neo-orthodoxy in this country there was the battlecry: Let the church be the church. This was too formal. It seemed empty to many.

Some three decades have now intervened, bringing great changes in our view of what this planet and our history are like. Today, then, there is need to stress: Let the church be the just church.

It may not seem much of a new discovery. And yet it does move us ahead in regard to what we have traditionally called the marks of the church (*notae ecclesiae*). Basically these marks have been the creedal ones. We confess the *one, holy, catholic, apostolic* church. What we are saying today is that faith in the church needs to be taught as faith in the one, *just*, catholic, apostolic church. If the *sancta ecclesia*, the holy church, is not the *justa ecclesia* (*justa* because of *justificatio*, that is, because of being made just) there is no point to holiness.

It is especially important in this context to view the impact of Messiah Jesus in terms of Matt. 6:33. Most theologies regard justice as something to be tacked on to the church somewhere down the road in ethical behavior. It functions in the field of ethics as a second or third step of theological thought. But it is not of the essence of the church, since it is not viewed as part of the function of Messiah Jesus in his community.

Today an either/or decision presents itself. It touches the jugular vein of much present spirituality in this country. In its 1977 Christmas issue, *Time* magazine's cover story was on "The New Empire of Faith"—the advance of the Evangelicals. Caveats were included. Carl F. H. Henry was quoted as saying, "Another year has passed in which the movement has registered no notable influence on the formative ideas and ideals of American culture."[8] Early in 1978, two thousand religious television and radio broadcasters gathered in Washington, D.C., with born-again *Hustler* editor Harry Flynt, Eldridge Cleaver, Anita Bryant, and Mrs. Bert Lance. One newspaper story covering the publicity-conscious meeting concluded with another caveat: "Evangelicals claim as many as 35 million born-again Christians, including the one in the White House. At the same time, however, many both inside and outside the evangelical movement warn that it must develop a social conscience and avoid the inward-turning tendencies of the Seventies, America's Selfishness Decade."[9]

It is easy to say that all the saintliness now being paraded around in public has been co-opted by the powers that be. It is understandable that people appeal to the need for developing social conscience as antidote. However, unless it is understood that Christians cannot but shape the *church* as social base for social conscience there is little hope for any appreciable formative influence of Christianity on American culture.

Obviously individuals can influence culture. But when the church as social base for Christians is co-opted by the powerful, so that it turns into an agent of the state legitimating injustice, Christians as individuals cannot have any influence except a negative one.

What is at stake here is the function of the church in the state. It becomes clearer every day that the church was never meant to be a self-contained religious organization hermetically sealed off from society. The church functions as an intermediate structure between individuals or smaller units of society (like the nuclear family) and the state. In some sense it is a buffer zone between the micro-units and the macro-unit. But our reference to new forms of socialism as a live option for us presses for something more specific. Obviously the church is not a socialist party. But the church is the antidote to solipsism and sheer individualism as well as collectivism. The issue in principle is the growth of genuine freedom. No effective freedom without justice! It is all very much in conflict with *Looking Out For Number 1.*

Socialism in the United States is under a cloud. It suggests communism and totalitarianism. One has to appeal to the historical record. We have to study again some of the more level-headed thinkers of the past on the subject. For example, no lesser mind than Martin Buber, in *Paths in Utopia*, made it clear how important it is to have a buffer zone between the individual and the state. He sees in socialism an important human effort to provide for such a zone: "The socialist idea points of necessity, even in Marx and Lenin, to the organic construction of a new society out of little societies inwardly bound together by common life and common work, and their associations. But neither in Marx nor Lenin does the idea give rise to any clear and consistent frame of reference for action."[10] A new society out of little societies! That is also what, in part, the church is about.

One has to understand that the church is also in the business of furthering "the withering away of the state." Time and again the state assumes much too much power over people. But that does not mean that the state will soon disappear. Martin Buber articulates the principle involved:

As to the problem of action Lenin starts off with a purely dialectical formula: "So long as there is a State there is no freedom. Once there is freedom there will be no more State." Such dialectics obscures the essential task, which is to test day by day what the maximum of freedom is that can and may be realized today; to test how much "State" is still necessary today, and always to draw the practical conclusions. In all probability there will never—so long as man is what he is—be "freedom" pure and simple, and there will be "State," i.e., compulsion, for just so long; the important thing, however, is the day to day question: no more State than is indispensable, no less freedom than is allowable. And freedom, socially speaking, means above all freedom for community, a community free and independent of State compulsion.[11]

The church is very much the community that seeks to be free and independent of state compulsion. But it cannot achieve such freedom today without grasping the socialist principle inherent in society. The East has developed it negatively in terms of state centralism. We in the West have a chance to develop it in terms of the de-centralization of state power. It is especially in the economic realm that the socialist principle becomes tangible. The church can be a witness to the possibilities of de-centralization. To appeal once more to Martin Buber: "An organic commonwealth . . . will never build itself up out of individuals but only out of small and ever smaller communities: a nation is a community to the degree that it is a community of communities."[12] The church today is on the way to understanding itself again as a community of communities—struggling over the embodiment of justice.

It is only within the context of a church, such as the United Church of Christ, struggling for justice that we get a clear notion of the emerging function of the church. Up to this point theology has not sufficiently immersed itself, together with the church, in the battles of history. To come back to the mark of the church called holiness, we read in the second edition of John Macquarrie's *Principles of Christian Theology* that: "Holiness is cooperation with the letting-be of Being, it is the strengthening and promoting of the beings against the threat of dissolution."[13] There are twelve pages in Macquarrie on the marks of the church. The issue of justice does not appear in specific terms. From the perspective of the "Liberation Affirmation," that specificity can no longer be avoided. Theology that keeps the church in a separate history outside the history of the human struggle is misleading.

John Macquarrie observes: "The visible embodiment of the Church's holiness is its sacramental life."[14] The sacramental life is indeed crucial. But it all depends on how we understand the basic character of the sacrament in history. Since Messiah Jesus is the embodiment of God's justice, his church is drawn into the struggle for justice as a matter of course. For the church, Messiah Jesus as the motivation of the justice struggle makes the sacraments the crucial witness to God's immersion *in history*. Water bears witness to the dying of Messiah Jesus in history. Bread and wine do the same.

In the Incarnation God enters history. Baptism in the Jordan belongs to it. Outside the city wall God consummates the Incarnation on the cross. Especially in Greek thought, God and the human being could not possibly enter into that close a relationship. So God's embodiment is another metaphor that paradoxically creates the new situation of history. The new event is about God's justice-rule among humankind, re-establishing God's right among the people, and reconstituting human right. Human usurpation of God's right had introduced injustice all around. God's just covenant with the first human couple had been botched. In the Justice Church, God reconstitutes this covenant. Here God gets to be right. And human beings get their right.

God's creation of the human being involves God's right on human cooperation (Macquarrie also uses the word; the issue is what specifically cooperation is all about). The human being is created as God's *co-worker* in justice. Human rights means the ability to be co-workers for justice with God. God is at work so that this should be possible everywhere. Macquarrie's interpretation of holiness leaves out this dimension, which is characteristic of much Protestant theology today.

It is, for example, in the context of a church like the United Church of Christ that the struggle for justice revamps the notion of the church as holy church: "God is at work in all nations to create a more just life." The sacrament cannot but bear witness to it. Incarnation, Cross, Resurrection: in all God is at work for human rights to prevail. Holiness is not excluded. But holiness is the *setting apart* that comes when a person battles for justice. It often means being scorned. The setting apart that is holiness is quite clear: "He was despised and rejected by men; a man of sorrows, and acquainted with grief; and as one from whom men hide their faces he was despised, and we esteemed him not" (Isa. 53:3).

The holiness of justice issues in forgiveness of sins and eternal life. Eternal life in our faith experience today as well as in the life to come is the final outcome of the battle for justice in history.

The sacramental understanding of the Incarnation as having an impact on history in an *ongoing* way is immediately pitted against all manner of injustice: "The church is called to be in constant conflict in various ways with principalities and powers that legitimate injustice." It is a profoundly simple equation. Since God is battling against injustice in history, the church cannot but also battle against injustice.

## LET CULTURE BE AN OBEDIENT CULTURE

In the United Church of Christ we are only beginning to understand the emerging new function of the church. It is an intermediate structure more on the side of society than the state. But it is not identical with society. In a sense, it could be a watchtower over the difference between society and state. On the turf of society we stand at a distance to the nation-states pitted against each other. And yet it is in society that the values of the states are shaped. The church along with society creates or re-creates values that either enhance human life or finally destroy us.

The impression dare not be given that theology in this context comes down to sheer ethical injunction. The depth of the mystery of God has to be reasoned through time and again. What we are zeroing in on is the creative power of biblical root metaphors to bring the justice church into being. Messiah Jesus is the one root metaphor, Incarnation is the other. We need to understand how the church comes to be. Loisy's idea that what was expected was the kingdom, what came was the church, reflects the irony of history. But in this case the irony of history makes a lot of sense. Messiah Jesus and Incarnation introduce dynamics of renewal into society. Society does not radically link life and justice. It finds all kinds of rationalizations for willfully inducing death, whether on the battlefield or in laboratories. The church comes about because God negates death as final. Without resurrection there is no church. Our human habit of letting death decide who is the strongest, the fittest, or the most "surviving," completely disregards justice. The dead have no human rights. As paradoxical as it may sound, the reason for the Incarnation is very simple: "God is battling death as the enemy of justice."

It has to be understood at this point that *God* is fighting the battle. Human beings are asked to join God. We will never be able to accomplish much while assuming it is we who are battling *for* others. The strength in recreating values lies in struggling *together with* God and *together with* others. If we do not struggle together with God here, we do not notice God at all. That is why God is so dead for many. God wants us to be creative co-workers in justice.

There is much built into our society in preconception, prejudice, and sheer technological happenstance that contradicts God's enhancement of life, for example, merchandizing of weaponry, export of war machinery, and nuclear proliferation. The probability of a nuclear holocaust is not lessening. The abortion question has not been settled in a life-affirming way. Each issue lends itself to a lengthy analysis. The main point we wanted to clarify was that theological reflection in the church on "the death dealings of our culture as well as other cultures" has to be tied to the excruciating experience of the poor and God's justice struggle for all suffering people. There is an increasing agreement among Christian churches on this point. Says Richard Neuhaus: "Justice must always be measured in terms of how it affects those at the bottom. This insistence is in line with the biblical emphasis upon the poor, the *anawim*, and their central role in the divine economy."[15]

With this premise of interdependency between the right to life and the struggle of the victimized, we now understand better how to approach an issue such as abortion. Again in the words of Richard Neuhaus:

> There is a further and serious concern that our society could become dominated by what some call an "abortion mentality." That is, public policy could be oriented in an increasingly anti-natalist direction. Then too, there is the danger of a superficially utilitarian approach to human life: that which is not useful is dispensable. Such an approach is utterly contrary to the Christian faith. Our society and all societies are measured in terms of the concern we evidence for the weakest, the poorest, and the most despised.[16]

All this does not mean that there are easy answers. But the resurrection is now believed in terms of life-affirming actions. With this kind of orientation, *every sermon becomes also a public policy statement*, calling for life-affirming public measures.

What we preach as God's struggle for the poor is very much related to God's struggle for the life of the fetus as well as the life of the mother. God's justice is the divine right on creative co-workers for justice. Obviously in this regard there is no absolute in sinful humanity. But the struggle in the church wherever God's justice is preached is over the divine right on human life that gives each person the right to life, the right to become a responsible person as co-worker for justice. So the church, we said, "is people working for an obedient culture in keeping with God's will."

What develops in the struggle between society and the church over creating and recreating values is culture. Obviously Christians dare not gather in church merely to enjoy their religion. The mandate of God's mission in the world for justice always asks the Christian to join God in the world. The result is not perfection but the mix of values called culture.

Church and culture stand in constant tension. It is not the task of the church, however, constantly to say "no" to the outcome of the creation and recreation of values. *Church against culture* is not a responsible Christian stance. But that is less and less the danger the churches face. The threat is the *church of culture* syndrome, the attitude of yielding to and legitimating the level of values attained today as culture. As the church has to become obedient time and again, so culture has to be reminded of the need for obedience on grounds of God's struggle for justice.

Here a difficult battle in scholarship is being joined. On the premise of Talcott Parsons' thesis that "secularization" has, essentially, taken the form of differentiation, John Murray Cuddihy points out that the denomination "is the last phase in the evolution of a differentiating Protestantism."[17] The issue that needs to be examined carefully is whether or not we have to accept this development as normative for the church. It is pointless to argue with history. The denomination is historically very real in North America. But there is no compelling reason why we should not ask whether or not the denomination contradicts the purpose of Christianity in the long run. Cuddihy is satisfied with the present stage of Christian value infusion in culture:

> It is a high irony of our culture that the current phase of Western civilization—especially in the Anglo-American area of "civic culture" and "civil religion"—which both secularists and religionists agree in calling "post-Christian society" is, for Talcott Parsons—as for me—a genuine, progressive stage in the further institutionalization of Christian values into the social structures and institutions (political, academic, economic, and other) of our society.[18]

So far so good, if it were not for the somewhat triumphant fiat that "by the roundabout route of differentiation, there now exists a more Christian society than ever before in history."[19]

I do not believe that as a counterargument one should point to the arms race, the billion-dollar military budgets, sex mores, or profit-seeking. It is rather the inherent need of Christian witness to stress that Christianity was not meant to create a "Christian society." If nothing else, the eschatological expectation in primitive Christianity of the near end excludes it. What is more, the normal sinfulness of the human race works counter to any "Christianizing" of the social order. So the church is confronted with the task of Sisyphus. With each generation, the call to a responsible culture begins all over again. Each generation has to be converted again to God.

Three corollaries of a position that tries to transcend a *church against culture* or a *church of culture* orientation need to be noted.

1. There is no reason to feel guilty. Cuddihy thinks that Christians feel "guilty" for not doing better, since the more responsibly Christian—individualistic, universalistic, idealistic, self-critical, concerned—society becomes, the more Christians feel they have failed and become post-Christian and secularized. Their sense of guilty failure is a direct consequence of the hypertrophy of upgraded demands they now make upon themselves and society. But the Christian will never face the finished product of a Christianized society. Because of sin, influencing society by Christian values is an unending task. Guilt has no place in this historical dynamic. We need not feel guilty for what we cannot do. The whole premise of an ever more Christian society needs to be scuttled. Of course in every generation society can be infused with a measure of Christian values. But society is also the great diluter of Christian values. So in each generation the Sisyphean task of infusing society with Christian values starts all over again.

2. There is no longer any reason to stress love as the core of the Protestant principle. When the notion prevails that Christian values are being more and more translated into society Christian love is increasingly domesticated and thus made innocuous. We need to decide whether the nature of Christianity is accurately portrayed if we take our cue from the cultural status quo. The civil religion argument, now refined by John Murray Cuddihy, answers in the positive:

> The Protestant phase sees *agape* institutionalized as courtesy-decency, retaining the structure of *agape,* extending it beyond the female principle, but tinging it slightly with the class condescension of the bourgeois era ("lady bountiful"). The denominational phase institutionalizes *agape* as civility. Gone, now, is the warm, caritative effect, but in its place is a wider *extension* of trust (taking the bourgeois-parliamentary form of "respect"). The trust of "respect" is

now a civil debt owed to *everyone*. Entitlement to respect and, if not to actual trust, at least to the "show" of trust we call "good faith" becomes universalized and upgraded.[20]

As to what is actually happening in church/society relationships in the United States, Cuddihy is right on target. The problem is that what *is*, the status quo, also becomes the norm. For the Justice Church "good faith" is great, but not decisive for "showing how to keep together a civilization." It is fundamental for the United Church of Christ to fight for the human rights of the Wilmington Ten on grounds of God's rights, so that not merely good faith is kept, but justice prevails. We are not merely to view the other in terms of respect, but in terms of God's claim expressed through the other. The State of North Carolina would relate differently to the Wilmington Ten if God's claim in the other were acknowledged.

3. There is also no longer any reason to succumb to modern differentiation as legitimation of denominationalism. The intrinsic mandate of Christianity is to share the claims of the other in the unity of all members of the church (cf. 1 Cor. 12:14–26). The stranglehold of modernity has taken North American Christianity mainly in the opposite direction. The United Church of Christ is an exception. There are others. COCU, the Consultation on Church Union, is an overarching promise of the new. We have to pay more attention in theology to these new developments. Obviously there is also ambiguity involved and we might develop only bigger denominational conglomerates. Yet without movement toward greater unity in embodying justice-love, Christianity will regress.

Cuddihy still reflects the conventional wisdom: "The civic culture becomes a community in which trust takes the form of the rites of civility, and in which the 'civilities' are the gifts that are exchanged and, in being exchanged, knit the members into the solidarity of a moral community, into a society (*Gesellschaft*) that is also a community (*Gemeinschaft*)."[21] Here the church as intermediate structure in society completely disappears, at least in terms of a significant contribution. But modern society (*Gesellschaft*) with class and group differentiations has proved almost completely incapable of community *(Gemeinschaft)*. The church is not the Savior in this dilemma. Yet it is God's ever renewed offer through Messiah Jesus to create community. Except for a community of justice that stands apart from culture there is no real possibility of the renewal of society. The task is to confront society with God's new reality time and again. The dissolution of the church into society has become a dogma we need to examine critically. With this framework in mind we say in Seminar I: "The church can be engaged with culture without being co-opted by culture as court chaplain of Civil Religion. Culture has no right to become the value-framework that determines the way of life in Christ."

## LET MINISTRY BE JUSTICE MINISTRY

There have been rumblings in theology for some time that before long in the church we would be entering the age of the Spirit. But all Christian theology is charismatic theology depending on the age of the Holy Spirit. The age of the Spirit arrives in history when the church fully realizes that God is ministering to us in history, "calling us to be daughters and sons," and thus to become co-workers in justice. Here each human being fully appears as person. The value of each person is affirmed only where the Spirit reigns as Spirit of justice. We become aware of it as God sensitizes our consciences to justice.

At this point a great shift is taking place in theology. We are moving beyond the radical monotheism of H. Richard Niebuhr and the radical Christocentrism of Karl Barth. In radical monotheism we are somehow caught up in general religiosity. Civil religion is here offered a good theological premise. In radical Christocentrism on the primary level we get caught up in an intellectual relationship to Christ. There are good reasons why for a lot of people it ended up in neo-orthodoxy. In charismatic theology, however, piety is subsumed under justice, thus making for a *church different from culture*. Sound teaching is subordinate to God's justice. There is no orthodoxy connected with it and no orthopraxis. It grows out of Christopraxis.

The Holy Spirit is not a mystifying reality. It is God continuing to work in history in keeping with the life, death, and resurrection of Messiah Jesus. The church is the place where the work of God as Spirit is brought to the attention of society. It confronts society with the power of renewal whenever it takes God as Spirit seriously, that is, when it takes God's justice seriously.

We need to stay within the context of how Christians today are trying to think through the justice task. A good case in point is the world hunger volume edited by Dieter T. Hessel, *Beyond Survival: Bread and Justice in Christian Perspective.* Three dimensions of justice are especially taken into account:

1. *Justice is treating people according to their merit.* Goods would be distributed according to some agreed-upon praiseworthy character or action. For example, we might decide to give more goods to people who make greater contributions to society or who show greater virtue or intelligence. We also might designate more goods for those of a certain race or family. All that would be required is that the standard be clear, not that it be "really just" on the basis of some other criteria.

2. *Justice is distributing goods equally among all human beings.* This is what Hardin has inaccurately called pure justice. It is no more "pure" than the other kinds of justice, just different. In this case, everyone, regardless of merit, would be entitled to a share.

3. *Justice is distributing goods among human beings on the basis of their need.* This notion of justice, often attributed to Karl Marx, is also very close to the requirements of Christian love.

Any Christian notion of justice will have to include considerations of more than one of these conceptions. Certainly, equality of access to goods and the assessment of the extent of needs would have to be included.[22]

The last sentence shows the Achilles heel of any definition of justice that leaves out God's justice. Assessment of the extent of needs? What is the criterion?

We need a further definition of justice, more precise in regard

to the theological base: *justice is human rights attained on the basis of
God's rights*. It includes rights to goods as well as rights to human
dignity. That is what ministry is all about; it is just that we have not
yet fully grasped it as the focus. In the end, the church has
nothing more to contribute to the human endeavor than God as
criterion of human need.

We forget too easily that human beings actually do not control
their own lives. Obviously there can be a lot of self-assertion and
self-liberation. But it all leads to enmity among human beings
pitting one individual against the other. "Doing one's own thing"
may bring a lot of self-satisfaction. But is it in keeping with the
destiny of humankind? The church in worship learns a different
dynamic: the momentum of history as God's own ministry,
"calling us to be daughters and sons," as Sound Teaching puts it.
The goal is the unity of the human family.[23] There has never been
a real unity. It still lies in the future. The criterion of human need
lies in the work of God that brings the unity of humankind.

The rights of God, as Creator of human beings, show in our
working for human rights. For the Christian the meaning of life
lies in sharing in this ministry of God: "Becoming daughters and
sons in turn involves worship of God that overcomes race, sex,
and class domination, making us sisters and brothers." Worship
in the end is about a very divine thing in a human thing. In this
plain way a signal is given in humankind to look for the unity of all
people.

"Re-creation of people through the Spirit affirms the value of
each person. God brings each a vision of life abundant. That life
issues in the discipline of piety in each individual Christian.
Human beings become persons where the Spirit of justice reigns."
The counterpoint for the renewal of society lies right here. There
is no other dynamic for the true renewal of society than the value
of the person once the human rights of this person are acknowledged. The affluent society, the consumer society, or even the
Great Society, cannot be models of the abundant life. Regardless
of what goes on around them, Christians choose a life of discipleship, a life of disciplined piety. But it is not the individual Christian who does the converting of society. It is first of all God who

keeps the pressure on. It is the Spirit of justice who makes human beings aware of themselves as persons.

In a strange way that Spirit of justice uses the church as corporate instrument to renew society. It happens that the Spirit rejects the church when the church does not respond to God as "empowering presence in history." So there is always an internal struggle in the church for renewal. This is what is happening in the United Church of Christ today. The point of using the seminar statement is not to present the United Church of Christ as a paragon of virtue. It is to indicate that the Spirit of justice evokes the dynamic of renewal in the church that has to be struggled for time and again in each denomination: "In Jesus Christ, God continues to draw near as Immanuel, God with us, so that the church can be a community of true worship among all people."

The root metaphors need to come alive as present empowerment of the church. In a sense, the Holy Spirit is God present in these root metaphors, vivifying people to be church — Spirit Covenant. But we need to understand how difficult renewal by the Holy Spirit is today. A whole superstructure of theological words has to collapse, so that we can see the simplicity of things "ecclesiastical." It comes down time and again to what God is doing in history: "God in ministry to the poor, outcast, and lost battles to order human history for the sake of justice and life."

The test of any North American liberation theology today is how a denomination as a whole can be sensitized to join in God's struggle for justice. The United Church of Christ has taken a few steps toward this goal. But we have to understand that it is a new goal. Our foremothers and forefathers sought to be faithful to their tasks. Faithfulness in our task involves a radical reorientation of all church members to personal immersion in history. The time of the church as retreat center is over: "Ministry and polity of the church become means of sharing in the struggle in a revolutionary as well as an orderly way."

Key to understanding the ministry of justice is its revolutionary dynamic. The church is set against those powers that keep people in fear of each other. God is putting down from their thrones the warlords and landlords — all overlords that keep people in bondage. The Gospel of forgiveness and redemption cannot be reconciled to injustice. The overthrow of unjust powers is part of the Gospel. The root metaphors of the Gospel compel us to shape ministry and polity in such a way that the unity of humankind becomes an inescapable goal. This emerging new function of the church determines the new function of theology. What it means in practical terms for the shaping of a denomination can best be expressed as an invitation: "The ministry of Word and Sacrament embodied in just polity seeks to evoke faithfulness to God's action in the lives of all people. The teaching office of the church, responsible for discipline and transformation, invites people to present their bodies as living sacrifices in the struggles of history."[24]

## NOTES

1. Martin E. Marty, "Denominations: Surviving the '70s," *Christian Century,* 94:42 (December 21, 1977), p. 1187.

2. Langdon Gilkey, *Reaping the Whirlwind: A Christian Interpretation of History* (New York, 1976), p. 46.

3. Quoted in Alfred Kazin, *On Native Grounds* (New York, 1970), p. 359.

4. We are here referring to Walter Rauschenbusch, *Christianity and the Social Crisis* (New York, 1910), pp. 151, 169, *passim.* Rauschenbusch premised much of his work on the notion of "the immense latent perfectibility in human nature" (p. 422). Chastened in two World Wars we have become more modest about perfectibility.

5. It was initially the intention of this chapter to speak of the liberation church. But a strange thing happened on the way to the chapter even within my own denomination. I wrote my book *Liberation Theology* (1972) also as a member of the United Church of Christ. To the best of my knowledge, it was in that book that the term "liberation church" was used for the first time in the North American context (pp. 174–224). Now it was time to make a more explicit effort in clarifying the use of the term. But it was already being used in contexts making quite different claims. I know how dated the book is. I was unaware of many things at the time. In my particular context the question of sexism was only looming on the horizon. But it makes little sense when in our denomination the impression is given that only now we are grasping the notion of the liberation

church: see Susan Savell, "Liberation Church Development," *A.D. 1978,* 7:3 (March 1978), pp. 46–48.

6. Reinhold Niebuhr, *Moral Man and Immoral Society* (New York, 1932), p. 57.

7. Ibid.

8. *Time,* December 26, 1977, p. 57.

9. *Durham Morning Herald,* January 22, 1978.

10. Martin Buber, *Paths in Utopia* (Boston, 1958), p. 99.

11. Ibid., p. 104.

12. Ibid., p. 136.

13. John Macquarrie, *Principles of Christian Theology* (New York, 1977), pp. 405f.

14. Ibid., p. 406.

15. Richard John Neuhaus, *Time Toward Home* (New York, 1975), p. 134.

16. Richard John Neuhaus, *Christian Faith and Public Policy* (Minneapolis, 1977), p. 116.

17. John Murray Cuddihy, *No Offense: Civil Religion and Protestant Taste* (New York, 1978), p. 17.

18. Ibid., p. 21.

19. Ibid.

20. Ibid., p. 23.

21. Ibid.

22. Dieter T. Hessel (ed.), *Beyond Survival: Bread and Justice in Christian Perspective* (New York, 1977), pp. 33f.

23. Ernst Lange, *Die ökumenische Utopie oder was bewegt die ökumenische Bewegung?* (Stuttgart/Berlin, 1972), p. 119.

24. The reflections on the Sacraments in this chapter helped me to deepen the method of liberation theology as *eucharistic method.* My paper prepared for the 1979 Annual Meeting of the American Academy of Religion elaborated this point for the first time on an experimental basis. The appearance of Tissa Balasuriya's *The Eucharist and Human Liberation* (Maryknoll, 1979) is a significant challenge in this regard. The possibilities of a new understanding of the function of the church in the light of the Eucharist are here greatly enhanced. Another very helpful book in the same vein is Monika K. Hellwig, *The Eucharist and the Hunger of the World* (New York and Paramus, 1976).

# Epilogue on Dialogue

"Do we remain in a state of ecclesiological deficit? What have been the costs? What are the thresholds to cross for a new grip on ecclesiology?" (Avery Post) These words of the president of the United Church of Christ at a small meeting of the denomination in April 1978 summarize the basic struggle of this book. It is fair to say that in the North American churches we have as yet little praxis of the new function of the church. Does the church understand itself as God's instrument in creating justice? We are backward in ecclesiology because we take ourselves for granted as churches—with few new questions asked about the function of the church.

The church is like a ship on the ocean where at times the captain changes course unexpectedly. God has changed course on us. Part of the price we pay for not paying attention to the change is that we do not know where we are. In a world becoming increasingly complex we are ignorant of our tasks.

Not all the tasks these chapters yield are new tasks. Some are perennial ones. But most of the old tasks appear in a new light. The tasks discussed are not the only ones, but they do make us concentrate our efforts more reasonably. One reason we do not get to the new function of the church is that we keep most of our theological tasks neatly separated. The whole syndrome of genitive theologies of the past few years is part of it. The theology of the death of God, the theology of revolution, the theology of play. . . .

We cannot farm out our divisions into separate commissions or task forces without seeing their theological interdependence. It is exactly the mutual involution of the divisions that we need to tackle as we try to answer Avery Post's question: "What are the thresholds to cross for a new grip on ecclesiology?"

As we select from the preceding chapters a few thresholds, we need to remember how they are all part of the same structure called church. They follow in a somewhat "logical" sequence as we try to consider them in terms of their common structure.

1. *The Race Division.* If we want the church to be an effective witness to justice in society we need to work harder at overcoming the ethnic divisions that keep the North American church segregated.[1] Our society wants us to be divided, so that the church cannot be a troubler of Israel. Power, of course, can always be met with brute power. What our society needs is a confronting of power with just power. The church can be the vanguard of just power. So it will make less and less sense to bring together largely white middle-class people in large church unions. The task of the church is to witness structurally to a new justice. Mergers need to make the minorities part of the justice mandate. The reason North American churches are still fairly closed to Third World struggles is obvious. Majorities and minorities are hermetically sealed off from each other in almost countless denominations that cannot see beyond their walls. We do not need a monolithic church. But we need a community of communities that can witness to society as a whole of human corporateness within a structure foreshadowing the unity of humankind.

2. *The Israel/Church Division.* We have never been able to overcome the ethnic or racial divisions in the church because we have never radically addressed what lies at the heart of the church's divisiveness: the relationship between Israel and the church. The ancient divisiveness grows out of a "holier than thou" attitude. The fissiparous denominational process and the racial divisions in which we are caught result from the unresolved separation of the church from Israel. Where Christian dialogue with Jews does not lie at the heart of the church's life, it is impossible to discover the contemporary function of the church. Christians are not the center of things spiritual. God is. And God may well have rejected the church in its present form. The Holocaust did not come about in a theological vacuum.

3. *The Liberalism Division.* Theological liberalism added another division. Intellectually there were those who wanted to classify the church within the societal enterprise as a cultural phenomenon. They were the "knowers" who thought they did not need Israel

for the church. The intellect was enough to comprehend Christianity. Schleiermacher excluded the Old Covenant from present theological relevance. The modernistic attitude kept the church from battling for God's justice among humankind—appearances notwithstanding. The main thing seemed the battle for intellectual relevance in harmony with culture. That left a lot of people not privileged to be intellectuals out in the cold.

4. *The Class Division.* As the division of the church from Israel was hidden behind a smokescreen, the internal divisions of society were also hidden by the church.[2] It took a person by the name of Karl Marx to expose the ideological smokescreen in this regard. But the churches did not learn their lesson any too well. They still have to realize in concrete detail what they contribute to the division of society in classes and what it will mean to structure themselves according to justice.

5. *The Male/Female Division.* As long as women are not in the church, we cannot expect nations to grant their rights. I have not made this dilemma a special point in the book, partly because of its all-inclusive character. But I hope it is clear that I have been mindful of it. It is not unimportant how we structure our language in regard to this split and how we make others aware of its implications in the power struggle. If we do not feel certain things throughout an entire argument, it makes little difference that we utter them. So I proceeded according to the rule, less would be more.

6. *The Third World/First World Division.* The comprehensive framework of all divisions is that between the rich and the poor nations. No longer does one have to go to great lengths to make other people or ourselves aware of it. If nothing else, our shrinking dollar proves only too realistically how we need to learn what otherwise we would not believe to be true. If we did not acknowledge the great discrepancies in wealth voluntarily, history is now dragging us into their very core. The issue becomes whether we want to be willing learners or whether in the survival mentality of lifeboat ethics we all the more refuse to be part of the human family.

Other divisions could have been mentioned, for example, the "fully productive" versus the handicapped. Everyone can discover them without much effort.

## CAN A LIBERAL THEOLOGY BE
## A LIBERATION THEOLOGY?

The kind of dialogue that one hopes will develop in regard to all divisions mentioned can perhaps best be tested in the division created by liberalism, the area tackled least thus far in the theological analysis of liberation in the United States. Liberalism usually wants to be rooted in nothing but human existence as such in terms of the starting point of theology. But where does anyone encounter human existence as such—except in the abstract thought of the theologian?

The frequent objection that liberation theology cannot originate in solidarity with the oppressed has to be subjected to the scrutiny of data. The first datum to be considered is Jesus as foundation of Christian theology. For too long Jesus has been presented as lone savior or, worse yet, mere mathematical point, historically altogether inaccessible. What has become clear once more in this century of unprecedented turmoil and careful historical analysis is that, as Adolf Deissmann put it in his great book, *Light From the Ancient East* (Eng. trans. 1927), the New Testament figures rise before us "from the multitude of the despised and forgotten," with Jesus foremost among them. Jesus never appears apart from the poor, the despised, the forgotten.

Much of liberal criticism of liberation theology reflects the dominance of western methodology in our churches. While in this country a small number of white males have felt the need to *respond* to liberation themes, there is still need to go to work on the "seismic shift" in methodology in the West itself and to replace it with a new methodology. Robert McAfee Brown has made an invaluable contribution in taking some steps beyond a mere response to liberation themes.[3] But there is further need for *internal* debate with the conventional wisdom of our theological method. The present book is an attempt to continue the rethinking of our western histories as regards theological methodology as we have applied it thus far.

In order to focus the first methodology step more clearly we probably need help from New Testament scholars in deepening the form-critical method. The church benefited greatly from the emergence of the form-critical history of the Gospel more than half a century ago. What we now need is a deepening of this history as a praxis-critical history of the Gospel (not*Formgeschichte des Evangeliums,* but *Praxisgeschichte des Evangeliums*). Martin Dibelius, among others, made it clear that the Gospels originated as collations of separate units of tradition, such as sermons or paradigms, formed over a period of at least three or four decades after Jesus' death and resurrection.[4] He tried to track down the literary laws responsible for the emergence of these small units.

The small units belong to the genre of "micro-literature" (*Klein-literatur*).[5] While great literature reflects the individual idiosyncracies and creative energies of a single author, micro-literature does not. Dibelius speaks specifically of the authors as "unknowns." Today we have to probe further and ask who these unknowns were and how their lifestyles shaped their literature. As early as 1909 Adolf Deissmann wrote: "Primitive Christianity, alike in its leading personalities and in the prepondering number of its adherents, was a movement of the lower classes. The water of life did not filter down from the upper level to the many and insignificant. . . . The first to drink of it were fainting stragglers from the great caravan of the unknown and the forgotten."[6]

These unknowns brought forth a certain style of communication and communion that reflects specific sociological realities. They created units of tradition according to conditions transcending the individual. It was not like today where literature is usually tied to paper. Specific life-situations called forth these units. Dibelius mentions mainly mission, cult, and catechesis. He claims that mission was the *occasion,* and that proclamation was the *means* of promulgating Jesus' memories among the disciples.[7]

Dibelius stresses that all people who want to understand the literary units created by nonliterary people have to examine their *lives* as well as their cult.[8] Unfortunately, in Dibelius's day the concern for life got somewhat lost in the form-critical shuffle. *Form* was what counted. One did not get close enough to *praxis.* Today much hinges on our grasp of the lifestyle of the primitive Christians, not just their literary style. Their lifestyle was the matrix in which the small literary units took shape. That lifestyle was praxis. The first Christians were followers of the Way. Behind a particular literary style lies a specific lifestyle.

If we leave out this dimension we get merely an emphasis on Jesus-kerygma, as in so much of recent liberal theology, as norm of Christian thought. But the Jesus-kerygma, the proclamation of the primitive Christian community, is merely one dimension of the total *Christopraxis*. The primitive Christians proclaimed their message within an elementary unity of thought and action that can best be expressed as praxis initiated and directed by Christ. It is discipleship at its deepest and most demanding challenge.

God invaded human life in Jesus of Nazareth, drawing into the divine activity those usually excluded from full participation in the covenant, "the fainting stragglers from the great caravan of the unknown and the forgotten." There lies tremendous theological significance in this history. God shows solidarity with the unknown and the forgotten, the poor, the oppressed. God offers justice to *all* people. No one is excluded; that was the point. Included now were those who had been excluded. The primitive Christians could never forget it. They drew into their number those who were similarly marginal.

Solidarity with the oppressed is thus not an afterthought for the theologian, but belongs to the first thought, the matrix of theology where the theologian encounters the theological subject, God personally. Christianity originated in part because God did not want anyone excluded from the divine justice.

The starting point of theology is not first of all *our* identification with the oppressed, which is very tenuous, dubious, and fragile. We are compelled to begin with *God's* solidarity with the oppressed and its implication for us. Obviously part of the task is to fuse God's solidarity with the oppressed in the Christopraxis of the primitive church with our present experience.

At least two aspects of liberal theology seem impossible to identify with liberation theology, as I understand it. (1) There is the imperious way in which God is often told who God can be, whether it is on Schleiermacher's terms or on Tillich's terms. Unless one begins with the God who in the poor Christ identifies with the oppressed, one is not speaking of God on Christian terms at all. (2) Liberalism makes progress only when it works with a peculiar kind of universals, those general principles that are necessary pre-conditions of thinking anything. We have, of course, to use universals. But we first of all need to discover the person these universals are generalizing about. Because of God's identification with the poor in Christ, universals for the Christian include the fate of the oppressed. If we do not take into account the poor as place of God's entry into the world, does not the generalization of freedom as key concept, for instance, only reinforce what the liberal has enough of anyway, that is, middle-class freedom?

We have very little experience as yet in dialogue in these matters in our churches. In controlled settings like the American Academy of Religion or the American Theological Society these things may seem somewhat debatable, but not in our denominational separations. In our denominations themselves liberation theology is either taboo or a bogeyman. A first step is the attempt of making the dilemmas more widely comprehensible and the issues more widely accessible, especially as regards the increasing bankruptcy of liberal theology.[9]

## SHARING IN THE DYNAMICS OF LIBERATION

There is no substitute for sharing in the dynamics of liberation itself in North America. It implies a long march through the actual struggles of society at the present time. A few years ago when a new theology appeared on the scene it was generally viewed as a fad programmed for quick obsolescence in a society attuned to obsolescence. One could not stand a theology lasting longer than three years. As a consequence, theologies were produced to last only three years. But now in the realization that we need to share in God's ongoing work of liberation the game of producing fad theologies is over. Liberation theology deals with God's persistent struggle for justice and the tenacious human struggle against oppression in the last quarter of the twentieth century. The dissemination of liberation thought will take time. We might as well go on the scale of A.D. 1980–2000. Even so, we will hardly have scratched the surface. We cannot hope to recover in 20 years what it took more than 200 years to lose, sometimes, I think, almost 2,000 years.

Meanwhile in praxis nonviolence is the only way we whites can hope to be credible in our liberation witness in North America begun in the early days of the Civil Rights struggle. The eighties will employ new tactics to throw us off in nonviolent action. But with a clear mind about the dynamics of God's liberation we shall overcome.

Two final questions follow from these deliberations almost as a matter of course. On our pilgrimage we need to know at least the most pristine lodestars by which we can orient ourselves. We need to understand clearly the function of the Bible and the function of doctrine.

*The Bible as Justice Empowerment?* Protestantism began by being oriented anew in the biblical Word. Much of the authority of the Bible for Protestants has eroded since. Even so, the Bible is still centrally placed in most of our churches. Today we can no longer begin with immediate assertions of authority. And yet all we know of the pristine justice dynamics of our Christian faith is contained in this book. The power for being the just church is mediated through this Word. The power for justice in our civilization gets its impetus here. What keeps human beings apart is injustice, the wrong we inflict upon each other by refusing to treat each other as equals. The realization of the dilemma is connected to listening to the biblical Word. But how all of us are empowered for justice by this Word is still a lesson to learn. The understandings mentioned earlier growing out of the wrestle with the praxis-history of the New Testament loom large in this respect. There are issues of scholarship we have not clearly dealt with as of yet.

*Justice Teaching?* The church obviously is involved in more than interpreting the Book. There are the doctrines that tradition offers us as having developed in dialogue with the Book. In accepting the power mediated through the biblical Word the challenge emerges of shaping doctrine anew.[10] What is the valency of Christian doctrine when it comes to justice? The ecumenical movement has taken great strides in the direction of clearer justice teaching. Yet much remains ineffective because individual denominations shrug off the power struggles Christians are caught up in. Only a strong concerted witness of all churches might bring change. For example, there is no more creative task for human beings today than disarmament. Here especially the divisions among the churches prove a diaster. Churches as a whole do not as yet act effectively as a catalyst for a new world of peace, although time and again there are gestures in that direction. In the end, it comes down to a frightening reality: we talk peace, but build bombs. Of course, not as individuals, but as societies. We talk disarmament, but walk in arms. The beginning of the eighties in the United States is a sign of where we are heading. Iran is a code-word for what we allow to happen. The Haitian boat-people are another code-word. As in Amos' day, the churches concentrate too much on worship as cult. The worship of God is not primarily a cult act. It is a justice act. For that to be grasped, the doctrine of the church needs to appear as justice teaching.[11]

History is intensifying the issues. But only under the pressures of history can we hope to come to our senses. We cannot hope to solve one justice task in isolation from other justice tasks—in the leisurely pace many of us have become accustomed to. Some national church bodies meet from one quadrennium to another. And even if they meet every year, the whole method of tackling justice mandates can no longer be mere God-talk. All justice mandates hang together in history. They invite corporate God-walk.

It would be a bad blunder if God as justice were understood to act only in the struggles over class, race, and sex. God acts in the lives of the handicapped, the emotionally disturbed, and the hermit as much as in the struggles of history as a whole. The point is that God does not act in the lives of the handicapped and the contemplative apart from these struggles. It is the same God who seeks to bring about justice among all and in all places.

It is in God-walk that we grasp any God-talk: "While we chatter or listen all our lives in a din of craving—jokes, anecdotes, novels, dreams, films, plays, songs, half the words of our days—we are satisfied only by the one short tale we feel to be true: History is the will of a just God who knows us" (Reynolds Price).

# NOTES

1. T. Howland Sanks, S.J., and Brian H. Smith, S.J., "Liberation Ecclesiology: Praxis, Theory, Praxis," *Theological Studies*, 38:1 (March 1977), p. 16. Our situation in North America is different from that of Latin America, since our denominations in principle do not suffer from alliances with the state in terms of official relationships. The separation of church and state makes for a different initial focus in social analysis. This does not mean that morally the churches are often not beholden to the state.

2. Ibid., pp. 35ff. Class struggle in Latin America is *the* focus of social analysis. For the North American situation it is one orientation point of the justice struggle.

3. Robert McAfee Brown, *Theology in a New Key: Responding to Liberation Themes* (Philadelphia, 1978). This is an utterly crucial book in the North American struggle of finding our own identity in the worldwide movement of liberation.

4. Martin Dibelius, *Die Formgeschichte des Evangeliums* (Tübingen, 1959).

5. Ibid., p. 7.

6. Adolf Deissmann, "Christianity and the Lower Classes," *Expositor*, 7 (1909), p. 224.

7. Dibelius, *Die Formgeschichte des Evangeliums*, p. 12.

8. Ibid., p. 8.

9. Often the question is raised whether liberation theology is not the same as the Social Gospel. There is a significant difference insofar as the Social Gospel was largely beholden to liberal theology. We have not as yet fully thought through all the drawbacks of the marriage between liberal theology and the Social Gospel. My experience has been that many people feel they have been "hoodwinked" by the Social Gospel. They draw back at the mention of the phrase. It promised more than it could deliver. The liberal premises seemed to be legitimating doing good for others while not changing oneself.

William H. Barnwell has recently written a moving appeal for building a new Social Gospel movement. One needs to remain self-critical, though. Liberation theology has a primal concern: changing the churches where we find ourselves. I believe here some either/or decisions will have to be made. Barnwell writes: "In the latter days of the civil rights movement many of the black leaders made a mistake, I think, when they told us whites to leave the fray and go back to work among our own people, for they are the ones that need the help." The problem was that once we went back to our own people, often in distant suburbs, we too easily forgot the injustices of society and went on to the other things that were not especially related" ("Cats in a Wood Stove: Reflections on Building a New Social Gospel Movement," *Christian Century*, 96:19 [May 23, 1979], p. 589.)

Of course, we want to take into account the human weakness of forgetting—including the forgetting of injustices. But unless those are changed who inflict injustice, unless the unjust structures are transformed, our "intruding into others' lives" (ibid.) might make us feel good, but not really alter the causes of the bloody mess. It was unwise to wait until black leaders told whites to get out of the fray. When we are engaged in battling oppressive structures, "getting into the fray" and "leaving the fray" are not live options in the first place. We are caught in the structures from the very beginning. We are fighting our own battle. The whole issue of the relationship between liberation theology and the Social Gospel has to be worked through very carefully as a specific topic of research. We might learn more fully that "the basic thrust of the Social Gospel was by no means radical. . . . One might even . . . refer to the Social Gospelers as 'the praying wing of Progressivism'" (Sydney E. Ahlstrom, *A Religious History of the American People* [New Haven and London, 1972], p. 804).

10. It is important to note that the need is understood also outside the confines of our society. Another attempt, besides the UCC Sound Teaching document, is the *Confession of Faith* of the Iglesia Presbiteriana-Reformada en Cuba (Havana, 1978).

11. It has been widely understood that this emphasis on the church has been characteristic from the very beginning of the attempt to see the significance of liberation theology in North America. See Robert E. Cushman, "Fifty years of Theology and Theological Education at Duke: Retrospect and Prospect," *The Duke Divinity School Review*, 42:1 (Winter 1977): "I think I am not far afield in judging that 'liberation theology' is a call to the Church and church people really to affirm their liberation, through Christ, from conformity and bondage to 'the mind of the world.' In addition to recalling the Apostle Paul to our attention in this way, Professor Herzog is underscoring what Luther was saying in the 16th century: Let God be God in the Church! In Herzog's view this is an urgently needed word for the hour among the established churches of the South" ( p. 21).

# *Appendix*

United Church of Christ
OFFICE FOR CHURCH LIFE AND LEADERSHIP
289 Park Avenue South
New York, N.Y. 10010
July, 1978

*Dear Colleague in Ministry:*

*The Office for Church Life and Leadership is pleased to share with you the enclosed document—"Toward the Task of Sound Teaching in the United Church of Christ."*

*The document is a report from a theological seminar which was convened by the Office and asked to reflect on the faith and ministry of the United Church of Christ in these times. It was the first of several theological seminars and consultations which the Office has sponsored as a means of facilitating theological discussion and with a view to engaging the church in theological dialogue.*

*The seminar's conversation was broadened in mid-1977 to include some thirty persons, who received and responded to a draft of the work then in process. Now the report comes to you with an invitation that you share in that broadening conversation.*

*Attached to the report are four "Suggestions for Use," which the Office hopes will provide you with ideas for engaging others in conversation around the issues addressed here.*

*The Office expresses thanks to the members of the seminar for their willingness to serve, and for the high dedication and integrity brought to the task.*

*It is our hope that your reading and use of the enclosed materials will be a contribution "Toward the Task of Sound Teaching in the United Church of Christ."*

*Sincerely,*
*Reuben A. Sheares, II*

# Seminar Report:
# Toward the Task of Sound Teaching
# in the United Church of Christ

## PREFACE

The Office for Church Life and Leadership in 1976 convened a theological seminar to reflect on the theology of the United Church of Christ, particularly as it relates to the faith and ministry of the church. That seminar, composed of minister teachers and conference and instrumentality leaders, has now fulfilled its initial mandate and herewith presents its report to the Office for Church Life and Leadership. The discussions of the seminar concerned questions of how the theological task of the church might be done in ways which would both enhance the church in its own identity, as well as energize and empower it for ministry.

Convinced as we are that our church, along with the American churches generally, is excessively accommodated to cultural values and perceptions, our thinking revolved around the conviction that the ministry of the church must become more intentional and disciplined in teaching the faith of the church, in valuing its theological tradition and in responding to the present place of the church in culture.

Our brief report which we here submit seeks to be faithful to the character of the United Church of Christ. On the one hand, it seeks to articulate those *substantive* concerns pressed upon us by our theological tradition to which we are all accountable. On the other hand, it seeks to initiate a *process* of engagement and exploration which might involve the whole church.

The seminar was gathered out of a sense of urgency in the church. It intended to address precisely those issues judged to be inescapable at the present time. We have not attempted to comment on all of the convictions and affirmations of Christian faith and life which we gladly profess and which have guided our work. Thus much has been left unstated.

Our work, rather, has been that properly of a seminar. That is, to explore some fresh areas of concern and hopefully to initiate a new discussion that may engage the whole church in a new act of faithfulness. Our seminar was invited to probe these issues, but in no way authorized to speak normatively in terms of a statement of faith.

Because of restrictions of time placed on the seminar, we have only a beginning on the issues we have sought to address. We have in our discussions reached the point of being clear about some implications and next steps which follow from the conclusions we have reached. Our thinking has concluded that faithful ethical reflection and action and the problems of sound teaching must be held together and both depend on the recovery of the teaching function of the pastoral office. Thus our report concludes with a suggestion of direction which may next be usefully and faithfully pursued.

A draft of our report was "farmed out" to some thirty members of the United Church of Christ from July to September 1977 for critical response. We are grateful for the thoroughness of the critiques we received. They greatly helped improve our final draft.

> *Walter Brueggemann*
> *(convenor)*
> *Paul Hammer*
> *Frederick Herzog*
> *Ralph Quellhorst*
> *Henry Rust*
> *Clyde Steckel*

Also involved, but not present in our final formulation:

> *Reuben Sheares*
> *James Smucker*
> *Max Stackhouse*
> *Peggy Way*

## THE HISTORICAL CONTEXT:
## 1957–1977, TWO DECADES OF CHURCH LIFE

In 1957, the United Church of Christ became a new denominational reality in the United States. The Congregational Christian and Evangelical and Reformed traditions of faith, combined with the social challenges posed by racial injustice, economic exploitation, war, imperialism, ecological crisis, and sexism during the years since 1957, have produced a church body seeking to live its faith by Christian presence and advocacy. Responsive action has tended to precede and take precedence over theological reflection.

During these same years, faithful congregations, pastors, and denominational leaders sought to work out the implications for belief and church order of the new denominational unity. They struggled to live and affirm a vigorous Christian presence in the midst of pressures to conform to cultural expectations that religion should sanctify the status quo.

As a result of these developments, the United Church of Christ is known (and respected or vilified) for its courageous and controversial stands on ecumenism, racial justice, war, women's rights, labor rights, broadcasting licenses, multi-national corporations, and gay rights. While these courageous denominational actions were undertaken with every good intention and a keen sense of what faith required in difficult times and in keeping with the traditions of vigorous social witness of the uniting denominations, the United Church of Christ also seems to have scattered its energies so frenetically in pursuing many new causes that an enervation of spirit and aimlessness have set in. The United Church of Christ, its people and pastors, worried about institutional maintenance and growth, is caught up in the search for identity.

It is a time of profound and subtle temptation. When we attempt to be reconciled with persons alienated by controversial stands and actions, and when we try to create a more viable church system, we *can* identify so closely with such cultural values as harmony, growth, and efficiency (and the reassurance they produce), that the faith of the church embodied in its practice becomes indistinguishable from American civil religion. When that happens, the teaching office of the ordained minister is reduced to public relations, efficient organization, and supportive comfort.

Reconciliation and institutional growth are surely not bad in themselves. Indeed, they are among the gifts of faithfulness, as well as disciplines required by faith. The church's professional leadership requires excellence in organizational skills. But reconciliation, growth, and efficiency must always be pursued in the service of faithful Christian life and witness, never as goals in themselves.

Times of profound temptation in the church are also times for discerning and claiming God's renewing call to faithful ministry. In this present time the questions of identity, faith, and the place of the ordained ministry are all powerful signs of an awareness that the renewal of the teaching office in the church is an urgent need and opportunity.

This survey of two decades of church practice in the United Church of Christ suggests an approach to sound teaching which includes three core dimensions: confessions of faith, polity in process, collegiality for accountability.

## THE PRESENT CONTEXT: UNITED CHURCH OF CHRIST NETWORK OF SOUND TEACHING

A. *Confessions of Faith.* Christian faith puts us in tension with our cultural settings, calling us to make judgments and to shape fresh formulations of sound teaching. We recognize the continuing validity of the historic statements of faith; yet for our day we need to interpret or amplify them. Since the language of historic creeds arises in particular cultural settings, our life as Christians calls us repeatedly to find new ways to express our faith. For that reason, we need to articulate some inescapable emphases now.

1. Faith confesses God's presence, purpose, and promise. God comes to us with love and justice in the midst of our lives and calls us to respond to God's will. God's coming imparts eternal life, both as a future promise and as a present reality for human life. God's purpose encounters us and our cultures with both transforming compassion and critical judgment.

2. Faith confesses God as creating, liberating, and healing reality. Faith in God as Creator proclaims creation as good. Yet our sin pits itself against God's creative work. Therefore, God as Liberator frees us most deeply and decisively in the life, death, and resurrection of Jesus Christ to establish our true humanity. At work in the world, God as Holy Spirit forms us as the community of the church to share God's creating, liberating, and healing work by living and witnessing to it.

3. Faith in God's presence, purpose, and promise, and in the threefold understanding of God, confesses its roots in and faithfulness to the biblical witnesses. God's action in history, witnessed to in the Scriptures, fulfilled in the life, death, and resurrection of Jesus Christ, proclaims a unique and compelling perspective to guide us in the meaning of our lives in history *and as it is promised.*

B. *Polity in Process.* We understand that confessions of faith are not free-floating formulations detached from the structures of human society. They are of one piece with a polity that reflects this faith in the context of human organizations. In the United Church of Christ this appears as a multiform network of relationships, still after two decades being shaped and reshaped.

1. Polity as church government functions among us in the United Church of Christ with democratic processes. No elitist hierarchy is authorized to determine the structures. Seeking to be guided by the Holy Spirit, we endeavor to shape the community to fulfill God's mission.

2. Yet, such a community involves ordered responsibility; and, historically in the traditions of the United Church of Christ, this has meant specific offices within the community to further its life and mission. Ecumenical engagement places us in accountable dialogue with the structural forms of a worldwide community of faith.

3. This dialogue reminds us of our continuing need for the function within our polity of *(a)* responsible "episcopacy" entrusted to oversee not only finances, programs, and the organizations, but also sound teaching of the church, and *(b)* a responsible teaching office of designated persons who, by sustained grappling with major theological issues, call the church to be faithful to its biblical heritage in performing its mission.

C. *Collegiality for Accountability.* Within the context of a distinct polity and concerned for the quality of human life in God's world, we seek to make creative and formative decisions time and again in the light of the gospel and in view of ever-changing societal challenges and dilemmas.

1. The church is called to make particular decisions as an outgrowth of dialogue between pastoral offices and laity in a theologically reflective process. On the one hand, the theological reflection of the whole church and all its members is important and is to be taken seriously. On the other hand, and at the same time, it is important that these be sustained, disciplined, and formal theological reflections. Theological work in the church depends upon serious dialogue between those two functions and neither may be neglected.

2. Pastors, in concert with laity under the guidance of the Holy Spirit, function as *(a)* stewards of tradition, *(b)* shapers of sound teaching, *(c)* clarifiers and interpreters of the present human condition, and *(d)* personal examples of faithfulness in daily life.

3. The church seeks to make creative and formative decisions under the guidance of the Holy Spirit, so that we are mutually accountable as pastors and laity to sound teaching. Just as Jesus Christ was the Teacher of the community, the disciples taught in his name with mutual accountability (see Acts 15:1–35).

4. Each member measures the responsibility for creative and formative decisions in interdependence between pastoral offices and laity. All are called to serve together as servants of God in our mission in the world.

## LIBERATION AFFIRMATION

The United Church of Christ is at a turning. Harsh issues of sound teaching are emerging that we can no longer dodge. Church and society are caught in increasing conflict. In this situation, God calls upon us to give a new account of our hope lest we be "tossed to and fro and carried about with every wind of doctrine" (Eph. 4:14).

The following emphases appear especially pertinent:

*God is Justice.* God is struggling with the poor, the outcast, and the lost for a just life. In Jesus Christ, God takes sides with the poor. God "has put down the mighty from their thrones, and exalted those of low degree" (Luke 1:52).

Faithful teaching excludes the unsound teaching that God is on our side, that of a rich and powerful nation. The | **God and State** |

meaning of life does not consist of a national defense of wealth, but of struggling with God for justice among all peoples. As a sociopolitical and socioeconomic institution, the church is implicated in the evils of the state. It is called to serve God, not the free enterprise system. Today, racism is the most powerful means of "capitalism" to denigrate human beings into non-persons. Sexism today is its most powerful means of assigning persons the status of minors. We need to work for alternate sociopolitical and socioeconomic models. New forms of "socialism," including responsible public ownership of the means of production, are live options also for us.

*Church is Justice Covenant.* The church is people called in covenant to join God's struggle for the new age of justice. Jesus Christ as embodiment of God's justice is our only motivation in the struggle for justice. "Seek first the kingdom of God and God's justice, and all other things shall be added to you" (Matt. 6:33). | **Church and State** |

Faithful teaching excludes the unsound teaching that the church can transform the nation when it allows itself to be co-opted by the powers that be. Attacked by increasing secularism in our Western nations, the church is called to be in constant conflict in various ways with principalities and powers that legitimate injustice. God is at work in all nations to create a more just life. But God's embodiment in Jesus Christ, and not the American way of life or Manifest Destiny, is the clue to human destiny. It is Jesus Christ who calls and directs his people in the conflict.

*God is Life.* God is battling death as the enemy of justice. In Jesus Christ, God provides the power of life over death. "I am the resurrection and the life" (John 11:25).

**God and Culture**

Faithful teaching excludes the unsound teaching that we ultimately control life in our technological culture. With our vast technological know-how, we can cause death a million times over in our "laboratories" without the majority of the people even being aware of the murder. Totalitarianism is not always discernible by outward emblems or uniforms. It also rules in the cover-up of our "death industry." Christian faith opposes the death dealings of our culture as well as other cultures.

*Church is Life Covenant.* The church is people drawing upon God's vast creativity in human life. Jesus Christ is Good News as empowerment for sharing the goodness of life—conquering the destructive evils of civilization. "Do not be conformed to the world, but be transformed by the renewal of your mind, that you may prove what is the will of God, what is good and acceptable and perfect" (Rom. 12:2).

**Church and Culture**

Faithful teaching excludes the unsound teaching that the task of the church is to critique culture without showing how to keep together a civilization. The church can be engaged with culture without being co-opted by culture as court chaplain of Civil Religion. Culture has no right to become the value framework that determines the way of life in Christ. God's rule is to be embodied in culture. Both collectivism and individualism work against God's rule. The church is people working for an obedient culture in keeping with God's will—an unending task.

*God is Spirit.* God forms in us a conscience accountable to justice and life for true worship. In Jesus Christ, the meaning of life is worship in spirit and truth. "God is Spirit, and they that worship must worship in spirit and truth" (John 4:24).

**God in Ministry**

Faithful teaching excludes the unsound teaching that everyone is an autonomous individual free to do his or her own thing. Worship is first of all God ministering to us, calling us to be daughters and sons. Becoming daughters and sons in turn involves worship of God that overcomes race, sex, and class domination, making us sisters and brothers. Re-creation of people through the Spirit affirms the value of each person. God brings each a vision of life abundant. That life issues in the discipline of piety in each individual Christian. Human beings become persons where the Spirit of justice reigns.

*Church is Spirit Covenant.* The church is people responding in obedience to God's Holy Spirit as empowering Presence in history. In Jesus Christ, God continues to draw near as Immanuel, God with us, so that the church can be a community of true worship among all people. "By the mercies of God . . . present your bodies a living sacrifice, holy and acceptable to God, which is your proper worship" (Rom. 12:1).

Faithful teaching excludes the unsound teaching that ministry and polity are merely incidental to the life of the church. God in ministry to the poor, outcast, and lost, battles to order human history for the sake of justice and life. Ministry and polity of the church become means of sharing in the struggle in a revolutionary as well as an orderly way. The ministry of Word and Sacrament embodied in just polity seeks to evoke faithfulness to God's action in the lives of all people. The teaching office of the church, responsible for discipline and transformation, invites people to present their bodies as a living sacrifice in the struggles of history.

> Church
> in
> Ministry

## IMPLICATIONS OF SOUND TEACHING

Our work leads us to articulate implications for future work. While we indicate three such areas for consideration, we are clear that they are not distinct and separable items. Rather, they are facets of the single agenda of sound teaching. Thus, any future exploration of these matters should take care to address them together and at the same time.

*Implications for the Tradition as Useful Past.* From working on an example of faithful teaching, it soon became obvious that it also implies reclaiming the tradition of teaching in which we stand. It is necessary to think through again the 1959 Statement of Faith, the Preamble of the Constitution, and the basic insights of the Protestant Reformers, as well as the ancient creeds. This will take as much or even more time than we could spend on these few pages. We are now moving directly into a new situation of dialogue between church theologians and the church as a whole. We need additional input from all segments of the church in reclaiming the tradition.

*Implications for the Pastoral Office.* The historic traditions of the United Church of Christ have affirmed both the pastor as teacher and the whole people of God as responsible for sound teaching and learning. A democratic polity and an identification with all people can be used to neglect or demean the special responsibilities of the pastor as teacher. The United Church of Christ, through the Office for Church Life and Leadership, conference staffs, association committees, and theological seminaries, needs to develop the implications of sound teaching for the pastoral office, and ways to implement them in calling, educating, and authorizing the ordained ministry.

*Ethical Implications.* Ethical decisions flow from the sound teaching of the church. The United Church of Christ, from its beginning, has been a community that has not flinched from ethical decisions. It is our anticipation nonetheless, in light of our strongly held interests and in light of our past history of bold decisions, that the United Church of Christ might now undertake a more sustained and disciplined process of ethical reflection fully informed by our theological tradition and accountable to a faithful teaching function.

Such a sustained process of ethical reflection must include at least two ingredients: (1) engagement of the whole church, and (2) disciplined accountability for and to our normative theological tradition. It is our hope that the beginnings in this direction made by the seminar might enable the church to deal with the problem of culture accommodation and respond more fully to the gospel.

## SUGGESTIONS FOR USE

This report represents the work of a group of persons from across the United Church of Christ who gathered to reflect on the theology of our church, particularly as it relates to the faith and ministry of the church. The Office for Church Life and Leadership convened this group. We, too, are concerned about how we understand ourselves as a church and how those understandings get played out in our life. The positions in this paper, however, are those of the Seminar participants and not necessarily those of the Office or its staff.

The Seminar Report is a professional paper, aimed at the professional leadership of the United Church of Christ. It is intended to stimulate conversation and reflection by those professionals as they carry out the role of pastor and of teacher. It is not intended to set norms or to be a definitive statement for the United Church of Christ on the issues addressed. Rather it is intended to probe and provoke. Our hope is that in considering the points of view expressed here, professionals will be aided in their own theological journeys and energized and empowered for their ministries.

These Suggestions for Use are primarily for conference staff as they work with professional leadership. They seek to assist that leadership to get in touch with the basic information and assumptions in the report and to explore some of the implications of those for their patterns of leadership in the United Church of Christ.

Each suggestion is a separate design and can be used alone. You can also combine them for a longer program or meeting. In all instances it is assumed that participants will have a copy of the Seminar Report.

## SUGGESTION I

GOAL: Familiarity with the content of the report
TIME: 1–1½ hours

| | |
|---|---|
| *10 minutes* | 1. Form four groups. Assign each group a section of the report: historical context, present context, liberation affirmation, implications. Ask each group to review its section and prepare to summarize the key points for the total group. |
| *15 minutes* | 2. The total group meets to hear the summary from each sub-group. Opportunity for clarifying questions is provided at the end of each report. |
| *10 minutes* | 3. The same groups get together again and complete charts similar to the one below. |

| Things in This Report with which I Am Comfortable | Things in This Report with which I Am Uncomfortable |
|---|---|
| | |
| | |
| | |

| | |
|---|---|
| *10 minutes* | 4. The total group discusses points of comfort and discomfort in a general, open discussion. (This is not a time for group reports.) |
| *15 minutes* | 5. Return to the same small groups and discuss the implications of the report for *(a)* my role as pastor |

and teacher, *(b)* education and worship in my congregation, *(c)* over-all pattern of life in my congregation.

*20 minutes*     6. Share implications in the total group. List key implications identified by groups.

*5 minutes*     7. Closing and summary

## SUGGESTION II

GOAL: Exploration of Liberation Affirmation Section of the seminar report

TIME: 1½–2 hours

*5 minutes*     1. Briefly introduce the report and give a summary of its content. Indicate that the focus will be on the Liberation Affirmation Section of the report.

*5 minutes*     2. Ask participants to form three small groups. Assign each group one of the emphases in the section: Justice, Life, Spirit.

*10 minutes*     3. In the small groups, focus on the assigned aspect (either Justice or Life or Spirit) of God. Ask the individuals to sit silently and reflect on their images, feelings or thoughts of God as Justice or Life or Spirit. It might be helpful for each silently to complete this sentence: When I think . . . feel . . . imagine God as———, I think . . . feel . . . imagine. . . .

*15 minutes*     4. Share reflections in the small groups. Make a list of key thoughts, feelings, and images identified.

*10 minutes*     5. Post lists and invite the total group to move around the room and read the lists. (This also might be a good time to get coffee.)

*10 minutes*     6. Provide an opportunity for general observations in the total group.

*20 minutes*     7. Return to the same small groups. Point out that the report proclaims that the church is a "now" expression of God as Justice, as Life, as Spirit; that it is a people covenanted to act that out in the present and future. Reflect on the following in relation to the focus (Justice, Life, Spirit) assigned earlier:

—In your experience of the United Church of
Christ, where is it behaving as————; where
should it be?

—What needs to be happening in your local
church if it is to be more fully a community
of————? in the United Church of Christ?

—How can we help the church to be more fully a
community of————?

*30 minutes*  8. Small groups share in the total group where a list is
developed:

| If the Church Is<br>Called to Be . . . | As a Church,<br>We Need to . . . | As pastor teacher,<br>I Need to . . . |
|---|---|---|
| Justice Covenant | | |
| Life Covenant | | |
| Spirit Covenant | | |

*5 minutes*  9. Closing and summary

## SUGGESTION III

GOAL: Understanding assumptions in the report about the source of
and responsibility for sound teaching and clarification of one's
opinions/feelings about them

TIME: Open-ended

A key assumption in the seminar report is that the Church is responsible for the faithfuls' sharing and saying of the faith tradition in a way
which preserves and transmits the key elements of that story from generation to generation. The report affirms that in our polity those key
elements of the faith story are entrusted to a "responsible episcopacy"
and to a "teaching office of designated persons who, by sustained grappling with major theological issues, call the church to its biblical heritage
in performing its mission."

At the same time, the report stresses the importance of the dialogue,
within the church, between clergy and laity about the tradition and the
decisions it calls forth. Dialogue is a critical element in the process of

defining the teaching and clarifying the ethical and covenantal implications of the tradition.

In the group, reflect on the assumptions (especially as they are spelled out in the preface, in the historical and present context sections and in the implications section).

1. Do you agree with these assumptions?
2. Are they consistent with your understanding of the church as the bearer of tradition?
3. How do you feel about the roles of clergy, of laity, and of the two together implied here?
4. How is the tension between tradition and present experience played out here?
5. What changes would you make in these assumptions?
6. What additional assumptions would you add?

## SUGGESTION IV

GOAL: Exploration of the seminar report from three perspectives
TIME: 1–1½ hours

*5 minutes +*
*(15 minutes*
*for reading)*

1. Introduce the report, giving background information and an overview. If persons have not read the report in advance, time should be given for them to read it individually at this point.

*10 minutes*

2. If the group is small, work together; if more than 10, form small groups of 4–5 persons. Explain that the report will be looked at from three perspectives:
   a. The first perspective will help in understanding the basic content of the report.
   b. The second perspective will help in understanding the concepts/assumptions which underlie the content of the report.
   c. The third perspective will help in examining some of the implications of the report for the group and for the United Church of Christ.
   The group (or sub-group) discusses the *first* perspective using the question-starters listed below:
   —How does the report characterize the United Church of Christ? What is the "profound and

subtle temptation" of which the United Church of
Christ needs to be aware? How does the report
seek to approach sound teaching in the United
Church of Christ? Why is the renewal of the teaching office in the United Church of Christ an urgent present need?
—What are the key elements in any confession of
faith? How is our polity related to our confession
of faith? Who is responsible for the definition,
transmission, and implication of teaching in the
church? What is the role of the Laos (clergy and
laity) in the teaching process?
—What are some ways that the report describes
God? How does the report define the church in
relation to the descriptions of God?
—What are some implications of sound teaching
outlined in the report?

*5 minutes*  3.* At the end of the alloted time, if there is more than
one group, invite the sub-group to "quick-share"
some comments from their group. This should
move relatively fast. It is a time for ventilation, not
for a repeat of the small group discussion.

*15 minutes*  4. Repeat step 2 using the question-starters below:
—What are the key ingredients in ministry in the
United Church of Christ? What are some tension
points between inwardness (institutional maintenance and growth) and outwardness (action/
caring/encounter in and with the world) expressed in that ministry? How does the United
Church of Christ live out that tension?
—How have and are we confessing our faith in the
United Church of Christ?
—What is the proper role of clergy and of laity in the
life of the United Church of Christ in the definition and transmission of the teaching tradition?
—What is faithful teaching? Who defines that? How
are we carrying that out with clarity and vigor?
What concepts of God and the church are
missing in the paper?

| | |
|---|---|
| *5 minutes* | 5.* Repeat step 3. This time invite each group to share *one* key insight from the discussion. Allow a brief opportunity for clarifying questions, but no long discussion. |
| *20 minutes* | 6. Repeat step 2, using the following perspective question-starters: |

—Where in your life experience and/or church experience have you known and identified God as Justice, as Life, as Spirit? Where have you known and identified the church as a covenant expression of those attributes?

—What are the implications of the report for the role of clergy and laity in the United Church of Christ?

—If it is true that the United Church of Christ has "scattered its energies so frenetically in pursuing new causes that an enervation of spirit and aimlessness have set in," what are you, as a professional leader, going to do about that?

—How will you change your leadership patterns and behavior because you have read and discussed this report?

—List the ways in which you participate in the definition of the teaching of the church and its transmission.

| | |
|---|---|
| *15 minutes* | 7.* Repeat step 3, only invite groups to raise a question that comes out of their discussion which they would like the whole group to discuss. The leader should assist and encourage the discussion within the allotted timeframe. |
| *5 minutes* | 8. Closing and summary |

*If there is only *one* group, omit steps 3, 5, 7.

# Index of Names

*Other Orbis books . . .*

## THE MEANING OF MISSION

*José Comblin*

"This very readable book has made me think, and I feel it will be useful for anyone dealing with their Christian role of mission and evangelism." *New Review of Books and Religion*
ISBN 0-88344-304-X CIP                                    *Cloth $6.95*

## THE GOSPEL OF PEACE AND JUSTICE

Catholic Social Teaching Since Pope John

*Presented by Joseph Gremillion*

"Especially valuable as a resource. The book brings together 22 documents containing the developing social teaching of the church from *Mater et Magistra* to Pope Paul's 1975 *Peace Day Message on Reconciliation.* I watched the intellectual excitement of students who used Gremillion's book in a justice and peace course I taught last summer, as they discovered a body of teaching on the issues they had defined as relevant. To read Gremillion's overview and prospectus, a meaty introductory essay of some 140 pages, is to be guided through the sea of social teaching by a remarkably adept navigator."
*National Catholic Reporter*
"An authoritative guide and study aid for concerned Catholics and others." *Library Journal*
ISBN 0-88344-165-9                                       *Cloth $15.95*
ISBN 0-88344-166-7                                        *Paper $8.95*

## THEOLOGY IN THE AMERICAS

Papers of the 1975 Detroit Conference

*Edited by Sergio Torres and John Eagleson*

"A pathbreaking book from and about a pathbreaking theological conference, *Theology in the Americas* makes a major contribution to ecumenical theology, Christian social ethics and liberation movements in dialogue." *Fellowship*
ISBN 0-88344-479-8 CIP                                   *Cloth $12.95*
ISBN 0-88344-476-3                                        *Paper $5.95*

## MARX AND THE BIBLE

*José Miranda*

"An inescapable book which raises more questions than it answers, which will satisfy few of us, but will not let us rest easily again. It is an attempt to utilize the best tradition of Scripture scholarship to understand the text when it is set in a context of human need and misery."

*Walter Brueggemann, in Interpretation*

ISBN 0-88344-306-6      *Cloth $8.95*
ISBN 0-88344-307-4      *Paper $4.95*

## BEING AND THE MESSIAH

The Message of Saint John

*José Miranda*

"This book could become the catalyst of a new debate on the Fourth Gospel. Johannine scholarship will hotly debate the 'terrifyingly revolutionary thesis that this world of contempt and oppression can be changed into a world of complete selflessness and unrestricted mutual assistance.' Cast in the framework of an analysis of contemporary philosophy, the volume will prove a classic of Latin American theology." *Frederick Herzog, Duke University Divinity School*

ISBN 0-88344-027-X CIP      *Cloth $8.95*
ISBN 0-88344-028-8      *Paper $4.95*

## THE GOSPEL IN SOLENTINAME

*Ernesto Cardenal*

"Upon reading this book, I want to do so many things—burn all my other books which at best seem like hay, soggy with mildew. I now know who (not what) is the church and how to celebrate church in the eucharist. The dialogues are intense, profound, radical. *The Gospel in Solentiname* calls us home."

*Carroll Stuhlmueller, National Catholic Reporter*

ISBN 0-88344-168-3      *Vol. 1 Cloth $6.95*
ISBN 0-88344-170-5      *Vol. 1 Paper $4.95*
ISBN 0-88344-167-5      *Vol. 2 Cloth $6.95*